THE ENGLISH LANGUAGE - IRISH STYLE

'As she do be spoke, proper, like, you know'

P.J. Flaherty

'Literature is a luxury, desirable, indeed
But Language is essential, in life, to succeed.'

© Copyright

P. J. Flaherty
Author and Publisher 1995

Printed by JayCee Printers, Galway.

ISBN: 0 9525760 0 7

This book is dedicated to a genial and witty and wonderful teacher of English, Seán McSweeney, who fostered the love of language and learning in tender minds; and whose perennial and cheery:

'Good Morning, chappies,
Lovely morning, what!'

would tease, and ease the Monday morning blues, of memory - long, long ago

- when I was a little fellow!

PJF

CONTENTS

i

PHONETIC SOUNDS

(Key to Pronunciation)

Vowels   ā ē ī ō ū   (mate, mete, mite, mote, mute, moot)
(hard)

Vowels   ă ĕ ĭ ŏ ŭ   (rack, (w)reck, rick, rock, ruck, rook)
(soft)

As in dictionaries, the mark (-) over a vowel denotes "hard" sound
and the mark (˘) over a vowel denotes "soft" sound.

Vowel sounds denoted by ⸱ may be pronounced either way; e.g. Ate
(Et - European way, or Āat - American way) also 'pătent', etc.

Consonants: b, ch, d, dh, g h, k, l, m, n, ng, p, ph, r, s, sh, t, tch, **th**,
v w, x, y, z, zh.

The consonant **th** presents considerable difficulty to the Irish palate
and tongue, especially in Dublin and Cork, where it is often
pronounced as **Dor De**, e.g. Dat, De, Dem, Dose.

INTRODUCTION

It would seem, from observation, that the standard of spoken and written English in Ireland has fallen dramatically in recent years.

The evidence of school teaching, essays, exams, radio, T.V., newspapers, politicians, and general everyday speech points to this.

George Bernard Shaw

It was once boasted by G.B. Shaw that the Irish could teach the English how to "speak properly" and certainly in the early days of Radio Éireann and public broadcasting in Ireland, the standard was high, attributable in large measure to R.T.E.'s Bart Bastable. "Queens English" was the obvious standard then, but nowadays vernacular "Irish English" seems to be the norm.

In Dáil Éireann (Parliament) the standard of speaking is poor, esp. by some rural members - the recording of Parliament on T.V. or Radio demonstrates this clearly. On the other hand, the standard of public speaking in Westminster, London, is excellent. And ironically, it seems that it is the self-consciousness and fear of error in the Irish psyche that contributes to this faltering, timid, staccato delivery. The English (people) speak naturally, unaffectedly, and unselfconsciously in a free, fearless way.

In our schools it would seem that the teaching of Shakespeare takes precedence over the teaching of basic spoken English. Indeed, some teachers are less than proficient in spoken English. Unfortunately, there is more emphasis on literature than on language in our schools. Surely we should learn to speak well before we aspire to the study of Shakespearean psychology. "Queens English" is not, anyway, admired in Ireland, partly for "imperial" reasons and also for its perceived "snob" values. While there is not really an immutable, objective standard in a language, "good English" is nevertheless a legitimate goal, for reasons of clarity and aestheticism in conventional communication.

The following are some of the common "variations" in the Irish dialect, not universally applying, but fairly typical nevertheless, even in the high echelons of Parliament and the media, and almost exclusively in the predominant Catholic, nationalist populace. All observations, corrections etc., herein are not in any way 'criticisms', as "standard" English itself is still evolving and therefore the various dialects have a legitimacy on that criterion of linguistic evolution. The "standard" is merely that obtaining **now** and **generally** subscribed to on grounds of grammar, logic, aesthetics and custom. "Proper" English, then, is as much about "good taste" as about objective rules or standards. Language is volatile, and "bad taste" may become "good taste" over time, and indeed it can be observed that a new standard is emerging in the U.S. Many Americans proudly say: "speak "American" man, O.K.?" And, who knows, but that with its world-wide mass-media influence, "American" English may eventually replace "English" English as the standard. For instance, most young people now say "Hi" instead of "hello". I think however, that "good taste" will always apply and that the purists and academics will safeguard traditional "standard" English, with perhaps some minor concessions, for a long time yet.

This book is intended as a handy reference text, or "reader" for media people, politicians, teachers, spokespersons, etc., as well as for the general public; but perhaps its primary application would be to formation or corrective therapy in schools.

Due to modern mass-communications, English is now "the world language", despite being in second place numerically to China's one billion population. And while "Chinese" has several dialects "standard" English is now being adopted worldwide, with national and provincial dialects slowly giving way. Because of universal media coverage even local news or speakers can be relayed around the globe today. So, in order to be understood, local people must speak in standard English, even if their normal tongue is colloquial; e.g.

'I was just **afther, like, havin' went** out to the cow byre, **like you know** when it happened, **like**.'

[It would have to become:-]

'I had just gone out to the cow byre when it happened'.

It is all the more important then, nowadays, that parents, teachers and the State Education System should endeavour to foster good speech practice. This is not to be seen as a "snob", "posh" or "pro-British" design, but rather the rational recognition that English is no longer her Majesty's "secret service", but the common, everyday "lingua franca" of the ..... world!

CHAPTER 1

'He was a **fierce horrible** nice fella altogether, and **herself** was **terrible** nice too, **like,** y'**know**'

How often have we heard expressions like these? It shows that despite centuries of English rule in Ireland, the Irish have maintained a certain "independence" of speech and thought. Her Majesty's "Queen's English" writ never ran "aisy" in Ireland. Perhaps one reason is that the Irish do not pride themselves on elocution, whereas the English do. An Irishman would feel that he'd be regarded as a "snob" or a show-off if he "spoke posh", so sub-consciously he prefers not to stand out from the crowd. In this way he avoids jealously and is better liked by his peers. An Irishman believes that modesty may demand the suppression of talent or individuality, while an Englishman flaunts it fearlessly, carelessly, proudly. Thus, an Irishman is self-conscious in expression, while the English speak spontaneously and with eloquence. And why not, it is their native language, while many Irish people are just a generation removed from Gaeilge or Gaelic or spoken Irish.

While the Irish idiom has its own validity - humour even, it is nevertheless desirable, presumably, in this age of mass-communication, to aspire to a common standard of "good English". "Good English" has evolved, and is still evolving. The standard is not immutable then, having developed through Germanic, Old English, Middle English. However, there are certain objective laws of construction and grammar and logic pertaining to good speech in any language. Good English then, in this sense, is a universal standard in the main. This book, in citing actual observed errors in everyday speech and the media, aims to be a useful and enjoyable reader for schools and the general public.

All of the "errors" related here have been heard and observed in daily life in Ireland, and especially on radio and T.V., the newspapers and from politicians. Indeed it is said that the standard of spoken English has declined over the years, even though we claim to be the best educated people in Europe?! While there was always "Irish English" in common use there was nevertheless, in the early days of R.T.E. and the media, and in schools, adherence to the official

1

standard in written and spoken English. Readers, announcers and presenters on Radio Éireann had necessarily to 'speak proper, like'. Nowadays, there is a more liberal approach, influenced considerably by slang, "americanisms" and "verbal shorthand" like "hi", "cheers", etc. etc. Anything goes now, and every day on the airwaves and in parliament we can hear "dis", "dat", "dese", "dose", sthrike, sthream etc, etc.

Of course, "Irishisms" are not without humour, e.g. the politician who said:-

'where the hand of man has never set foot' or
'if he were alive today he'd turn in his grave'.

Teachers, in correcting exam. papers can build up a store of these gems, and many are used here by this author. But the "joke" might actually be on the teachers (some) (and parents) who should be the educators of these children, who, after all, only repeat what they hear from adults. Some errors are so ingrained, e.g. "I seen", "I done", that one wonders do teachers always know, themselves. It seems rather presumptuous to teach Shakespeare without first having taught students to 'speak proper, like, y'know.'

There was a full attendance in Dáil Éireann in 1963 when President J.F. Kennedy addressed the House. J.F.K. was an

accomplished speaker and it was said that many members were there to see "how it was done". Of course there was no great secret about effective public speaking, J.F.K. was just being natural and "himself", unaffected and unself-conscious. Irish people are painfully self-conscious and afraid of error, thus, even in Parliament, they tend to **read** speeches or deliver a rehearsed or memorised piece, instead of speaking naturally and spontaneously and easily. This has to be a cultural, not a personal failing, as J.F.K. was Irish too but spoke with universal ease, and extemporaneously, as well!

J.F. Kennedy

Irish politics (the theatre of rhetoric) has had few outstanding speakers, whereas **every** British M.P. seems to be masterful. James

Dillon, John Kelly and Garret Fitzgerald of Fine Gael were excellent performers in the House, while Michael D. Higgins, Conor Cruise O'Brien, Mary Robinson and others were adept for the Labour Party. The other Party has had few eloquent orators - even though some are coached by a professional P.R. company. If a person is sincere, honest, concerned and committed (s)he will be more spontaneous, less self-conscious, and therefore be a more effective speaker.

Michael D. Higgins

There is a false sense of modesty, humility and shyness in Ireland, whereby even an eloquent speaker is reluctant to "show off" his talent. Talent is God-given and should not be suppressed. We care **too much** about what others will think of us. The British do not and thus produce virtuoso performances in eloquence every time!

Professor Tomás De Bhaldraithe of U.C.D. in a preface to the Collins English Dictionary says that:

> 'All the varieties of English currently heard in Ireland have their origins in the Elizabethan period, and are based mainly on the north-west Midlands dialects of England.
>
> It started in the Pale and spread radially, but only as far north as the Ulster border, and encroached everywhere on the native Gaelic. Ironically, it was the Gaelic that stopped its spread at the border. (Gaelic Ulster!?)
>
> Midlands English did however reach Ulster, but via Belfast and the Lagan Valley, not by the Dublin Pale. Any differences in English North and South today arise from differences in **Gaelic**, which influenced English here. Syntactic peculiarities shared by North and South are seen in:-
>
> He is just **after** finishing his work;
>
> She has a desperate cold **on her**
>
> I have a terrible **drought** (thirst) **on me**
>
> 'All of these arise from a literal translation of the Gaelic. We now call it Anglo-Irish or Irish English. Northern Anglo-Irish was considerably influenced by its contacts with lowland

3

Scottish dialects during the Jacobean period, sometimes called Scotch-Irish, and lacking the southern Irish brogue. Thus, for example, a left-handed person is called a **clootie** in the North and a **ciotóg** in the South; and Southerners have a conspicuous pronunciation trait in often pronouncing **th** as **d** or **t**, e.g. **then** and **thin** = **den** and **tin**, while Ulster speakers maintain the usual English fricatives. An interesting feature of the English of most parts of Ireland is the survival of pronunciations characteristic of earlier stages of development of the language in England. We can instance: soldier, pronounced "soldcher" here, dew - jew.' "ye" for "you", etc.'

Some experts say that it doesn't matter how we speak as long as we are understood; i.e. there are no rules. But is it not because of rules that we **are** understood? Here are some examples: It is often said of politicians that they waffle, wiggle and waver, leaving the listener empty and baffled. This is because they often avoid answering the question asked, but answer something else entirely - a **rule** well known to every student: 'answer **only** what is asked.' Also, they often don't finish a sentence or line of thought, so that they cannot be understood. (deliberately?) If delivery is not properly constructed according to rules of grammar, syntax etc. it will not be coherent or intelligible to the hearer. A first rule here must be: do you know what you want to say? Then finish that thought or idea or point or sense through to its logical conclusion. Do not change your thought or train midstream, even if a new or better thought has hit you mid-sentence. You can always follow with the new thought later, in a logical sequence.

Once your ideas and thoughts are clear to yourself, and your delivery is continuous and coherent, its full intelligibility to the listener can still be ensured only if the **rules** of grammar and syntax are observed, e.g.

    (a) 'A pair of leather ladies' gloves'
    (b) 'A pair of ladies' leather gloves'
    (c) 'A ladies' leather pair of gloves'
    (d) 'A ladies' pair of leather gloves'

There is a different emphasis (or can be) in each phrase so how is the listener/reader to know what you intend? (a) might suggest that it is the lady who is made of leather. So, **rules are** important for clarity and understanding.

Therefore, while "standard" English (Queen's English) may not be fixed for all time (note the progression from Germanic to Old English to Middle English to Modern) it is nevertheless fairly certain that the present rules governing correct spoken and written English will always apply. Due to satellite communication worldwide, English has now become the "official" medium; provincial and national dialects are becoming more "standardised"; basically, Americans and Europeans; Africans, and East Indians; Australians and Scandinavians speak the same language now. The "standard" is therefore what is universally accepted, now, the late 20th C.

While "Americanisms' and slang are continuously assaulting the citadel of "proper English", and some of this is being assimilated, it is, thankfully, not replacing "proper" English, but merely expanding the vocabulary. The core value system of standard English is still

Pádraic Pearse

intact. We may use the "lingo", "hi", "O.K", etc. informally, but we still know the "proper" code.

Because of the current universal use of English, it is more important than ever that we speak the language well. This is not just that we may be properly understood but also that our communication is aesthetically pleasing to the ear. This has nothing to do with "accent", but more with proper, easy, clear, coherent delivery.

Thus it is that **language** should be the priority part of English-teaching in our schools. However, judging by the level of proficiency displayed by our politicians and by the media, it is apparent that **literature** and exams take precedence in our schools. It is surely absurd that the tender minds of our teenagers are being burdened with the mediaeval texts and philosophical complexities of Shakespeare, before first becoming proficient in speech and writing. Even mature adults find Shakespeare grave and perplexing, and apart from the occasional "To be or not to be" how many defer to Shakespeare afterwards? Most flee in terror from the spectre of Shakespearean psychology.

Very many good teachers of English share this opinion - and have expressed it on radio etc. Education, ideally, should be liberal, and for its own sake, according to the minds of Newman, Pearse, etc. The exam system tends to coarsen education, and make it a selfish, personal points-scoring exercise. If a student is studying merely in order to pass an exam, then the whole purpose of learning is lost. Learning should be for **love**, not for **tests**.

Anyway, if the exam system must still be maintained, at least the emphasis in English should be switched from Literature to Language. Of course this should begin at Primary School and in the home, for if a child develops the habit of saying: I **done**, I **seen** etc., it is difficult to change that by the time (s)he reaches Secondary School.

The hundreds of examples from daily use cited here suggests that language is being neglected. Paradoxically, we claim to be the best educated people in Europe today, but 30 years ago we had a higher standard of spoken English in Parliament, on Radio and T.V. and in the written word in newspapers. The U.S.A. found that with the advent of T.V., videos, and the **visual** media, that the verbal and written levels declined - even among **teachers**! Could this affliction be reaching our shores? We have been warned! The remedy is there. But do we recognize the malady?

GREETINGS: Lets begin at the beginning. Our first utterance every day is usually a greeting, e.g. 'Good morning'! 'How are you'! Common slang nowadays has Hi! or How'ya! the Irish are fond of **asking** 'how are you'. And the reply is often, 'oh, not too bad, like y'know, but the ould hip is bothering me' And yourself?

'Oh not too bad, like, y'know, could be worse, no use complainin', ha?'

Now this is unnecessarily garrulous and can become tedious if repeated over and over again - as with a presenter on Radio receiving several callers to the programme with: "how are you?" The point to be made here is that the greeting 'how are you' is **not** a **question** and certainly not a medical enquiry. It is meant to be a greeting, to be replied to in kind, eg. 'How are you!' Reply: 'How are you'. What is really being said is 'hello', so the response is also 'hello', as 'Hi' is to 'Hi' or 'how'ya' to 'how'ya'. The British say: How do you do! and reply in kind. "How do you do". Australians say: "G'day", with like response. Now, there is considerable confusion here as to the appropriate greetings and responses for the different times of the day, e.g. 'good morning', 'good afternoon'.

We often say "good evening" as early as 2 p.m., and "goodnight" in the evening.

The accepted, correct procedure is as follows:-

From 12 midnight to 12 midday: - 'Good Morning', response 'Good Morning'

12 midday to 6 p.m.:- 'Good Afternoon', response 'Good Afternoon'.

6 p.m. to 12 midnight:- 'Good Evening', response 'Good Evening'.

In short it is 'Hello', response 'Hello'. Now, the above apply to **instant** greetings when people meet, in which the response is the very same as the greeting.

This is not however, meant to apply in a time-lapse situation, such as a monologue, speech, radio or T.V. programme. In this case it should be an 'Hello', response 'Goodbye' situation. But, on R.T.E., presenters often repeat the opening greeting at the end, e.g. 'Good Morning' at start of the programme, and "Good Morning" at the end of the programme. This is like saying 'hello' at the end, instead of 'goodbye'.

Therefore, if the speaker/presenter opens the programme

with 'Good Morning' he should finish with "Good Day" (ie. if (s)he is not doing a 24 hour Ulysses reading). The same applies in the afternoon. In the evening, if the speaker is finished for the day, (s)he should say 'goodnight' at the end. If not finished (s)he might say 'goodbye'. If you finish a speech, programme etc. with the same greeting as at the start, then you are in effect finishing with an 'hello' when it should be 'goodbye'. Anyway, people/presenters can simply say 'hello' and "goodbye"; and if in doubt, they should certainly do so. I have heard a presenter say "Goodnight" at start of programme and "Good Evening" at finish!

12 Midnight - 6 a.m. If a conversation or programme on Radio/T.V. carries on past midnight, and someone calls, then it is proper to greet with "Good Evening" and end with "Goodnight" if the person(s) has not yet gone to bed.

If however, in the same period, it is understood that the caller has got up early, then the greeting should be "Good Morning" at the start, and "Good Day" or "Goodbye" at the end, because it is then **a new day** (morning) for that particular person.

On B.B.C. World Service Radio the presenters use only the terms 'hello' and 'goodbye' because of global time variations worldwide. And if in doubt, you too should use the simple 'hello' and 'goodbye', always correct and applicable. [By the logic of the above rules it would seem correct, between 24.00 - 6 a.m. to greet with 'goodnight' and respond with 'good morning' but this is not the accepted practice]. Indeed the practice is more often the reverse - i.e. Good Evening! at start, and Goodnight! at end; because it is likely that the audience are still up or about to retire to bed for a "night's" sleep - even at 3 a.m. If, however, between midnight and 6 a.m. it is known by the speaker/presenter that the guest or audience is already up out of bed for the **new day**, then the greetings should be "Good Morning" at start and "Good Day" at end - not "Good Morning" repeated, as this would be tantamount to saying "hello" at the end. Generally speaking "Good Morning" means "Hello" at all times, and "Goodnight" is wrong, even after midnight, "Goodnight" always means "Goodbye".

After midnight the greeting on the street should be Good Evening or Good Morning - I have heard "Good Evening" on BBC Radio. Again however, "Hello" and "Goodbye" are always in vogue and always acceptable. "Goodbye" is the corruption of the Middle English greeting "God be with ye" - which ironically must have been then an "Hello" - as is still the Gaelic greeting "Dia Dhuit" (God be with you, or to you).

This "hello" - "goodbye" paradox as evolved through the centuries neatly illustrates the truth that "standard" English is evolutionary, and that the "standard" is not immutable entirely, but partly 'the order or custom of the day'.

CHAPTER 2

MEDIA BLOOMERS

Local Schools can Speak as Good as Any

"Newspaper, Jan. 1995"

*'The Traffic **Corpse** arrived to investigate'*

'The losing team are coming off with their heads between their legs'

'De(e) eminent clergyman is a well-known tinker'. (thinker).

MEDIA "BLOOMERS'

Bloomers; Bloopers and Blunders.

An Irish political party employs a P.R. Company to groom its leading Ministers and Members in public speaking, appearance, dress etc.; and presumably it is a pre-requisite for R.T.E. Radio and T.V. personnel to be proficient in English (it certainly was in the old Raidio Éireann days). Yet, the following is a list of utterances recorded randomly and occasionally over the past 5 years from politicians, from T.V. and Radio 1 and sometimes from newspapers.
(Now, they may be citing someone else's script or speech).
[These examples can serve as an Exercise for schools (Corrections in Chapter 3.....]

At the outset, the most common anomaly, repeated daily, is with - greetings, e.g. On phone-in programmes, the callers keep repeating 'how are you' and the presenter may continually reply 'fine, thank you' or 'not too bad'. Now, surely once is enough to reply 'fine, thank you' as 'how are you' is not meant to be a health enquiry. The British say 'How do you do' and reply in kind. Even simpler is the word 'Hello!' This point is repeatedly made here, for emphasis.

Also, presenters, at start of programmes say, correctly, "Good Morning", Good Afternoon", "Good Evening", but at the end of the programmes some repeat the initial greeting. This is like saying "hello" again instead of "goodbye". Indeed, if in doubt, why don't programme presenters simply say "hello" and "goodbye". Simplicity is not necessarily stupidity. This brings to mind the following: I once visited a house at **8 p.m.** [N.B. Evening]. The woman was cooking dinner, but, being eager to impress, and considering the word "dinner" rather common, she said that she was busy, cooking **LUNCH.**

Chronology of utterances, as observed through the media:
[All Radio quotes are from R.T.E. Radio 1] from 1990 to 1995.

1990   **Will** I read it? ... We'll **speak** to each other about it
        (see notes P. 30) - Radio presenter.

1990   **De, Dese, Dem, Dat, Dose,** each **udder** - Radio presenter.

1990   I **pott** it down on my **fott, I tok** the **bok** out - Radio presenter.
        The two of them looked at **one another** - General Use.
        Secetry - common mispronunciation on R.T.E.
        I was **speaking with** him - new lingo, General Use.
        I could have **went** - fairly common.

Oct 90 **Fermenting** violence - reporter on Radio 1
        You **can't** smoke; from **half one** to two o'clock.
        He could **only pick** one winner.
        Good **Evening** (at 4 p.m.). I **seen, I done.**

1990   "Good Night" (at start of programme) - Radio, T.V.
        Commonly used in rural Ireland as first greeting.

June 90 **Robbing** antiques and metals .... at **half eleven** - Radio 1.

Sept 90 **Wemen** and men .... **dezision** (decision) - News T.V.

Oct 90 His running shoes were **robbed** - "It says in Papers" - Radio 1.

Oct 90 **Charless** Haughey, **tuh** ring, I **rung** the place **two times**
        - Today Tonight.
        I would have **rang** - Politician.

Oct 90 That's all from "Today **Tonight**" for **tonight,** so until
        tomorrow **night,** good**night!** - T.V.

Jan 91 Princess Anne's paternity (suite) **(sweet)** v Mark Phillips
        - Radio 1.

1991   Sportswriters/readers have a new tendency to say a

13

"fortuitous" score for "fortunate" score.

Oct 91   The **perceptive** that F.F. was responsible for Semi-State
        scandals .... - Politician (said it twice).

Oct 91   The estimates had **overran** - Politician, Radio 1.
        Den he told **dem** that he was in court for **robbing** a
        lawnmower - reporter on G.B. Show.

Oct 91   On alter**native** Saturdays .... not much **umour** - Presenter,
        Radio 1.
        The **Forward** of the book - Presenter, Radio.

Nov 91 **Mitigate** against - F.F. T.D.

Nov 91 A lady phoned a Radio 1 Talk Show and said that
        two Ministers in Government used bad grammar.

Nov 91 On a morning Radio Competition nearly all 5
        contestants used bad grammar: e.g. 'it was fantastic'
        repeatedly; "how and ever", 'we use this one **either**'; 'de, dat,
        dose', 'in the **centre** of the bed' '**tree** -foot wide bed' '**umerous**'
        the **udder** judge'.

Nov 91 On the Pat Kenny Radio Show a political correspondent said
        that a Government Minister would need elocution.
        9 p.m. T.V. News, Reporter said inte**rest**ed i.e. stressed the
        middle vowel section.

Nov 91 A writer and broadcaster rang G.B. Show about bad political
        English - e.g. one politician said that he made the "ultimate"
        sacrifice (death?).
        He will **rise** the castle again (Slane) - Radio Presenter.
        Trill seeker - Radio Presenter.
        A person rang Pat Kenny on radio to ask which was right
        "Mary and I" or 'Mary and me" (of course both are right,
        depending on their Cases).

Nov 92 Having my hand **shook** - Advert on Radio 1.

Oct 91 'Holloween' - Advertiser on Radio and T.V.

May 92 'Holloween' - Radio and T.V. Presenter.

Jan 92 He is **terribly** nice - L.L. Show.

Mar 92 It will become more **patchier** - Weather presenter.

Mar 92 Instead of **us** doing it - Radio 1 presenter.

Nov 92 Divide regions between **each other; disassociated, often times** (archaic) - Politician.

May 92 'Myself and John' Politician and a **teacher.**
When you see himself and his band - Radio presenter.
Sand **doons** in Portmarnock - Newsreader. [Americanism]

May 92 There are **less** wild men here now - A Professor.

1992 The Bishop of Kerry had no objection to **me** coming here - Politician on Radio 1.

May 92 **Rarin** to go - Some newspapers, repeatedly.

May 92 A presenter on R.T.E. thought that St. Jude was a **woman.** He said he couldn't read **"Peruvian"**.

May 92 **Francis** Fitzgerald on a woman's picture - In a newspaper.
Fortuitously, the 17th Hole is close by - T.V. - Carrolls Golf.
He **disected** the fairway - T.V. - Carrolls Golf.

Q.   Do you mean to say that you were not there?
A.   No! I was miles away. - Radio 1.

Residence Association - Common.

June 92 The **richesness** of Joyce - Politician.
A number of **referendas** - Politician.

Feb 92 Two complem**ent**ary tickets - (typed letter). Common.
Robbed my savings - Advert on Radio.

Dec 92 Harp **larger** (lager) - T.V. Advert.

June 92 It can only be successful **but** on that basis that ....
Revenue collection is based on **thrust**
De audit shows .... Politician.
He showed great **cunningness** - common.

June 92 Till all **entrances** are checked for the Round Ireland
Sailing Race - News Presenter.

July 92 A caller on Radio 1: He **seen** the Kremlin.

July 92 José Carreras **sung** beautifully - Radio presenter.

Oct 92 Arsenal **sunk** Forest - Radio Sports presenter.

June 92 He's first win of the season. He got **beat** - Sports Stadium

June 92 "**Disassociated** himself" - Radio 1 News.

Oct 92 Had I not **went** - Teacher of English on L.L.S.

June 92 Between **you** reading it and **me** talking about it - Radio 1.

July 92 There are so many new buildings have gone up - T.V. -
University Professor.

Aug 92 Bought **off** him - T.V. 9 p.m. News presenter.

Oct 92 Ines**teem**able value - 9 p.m. News presenter.

Oct 92 America and Canada - Arts Show - 7.01 Radio.
Incidentences - person being interviewed 7.01 Radio.

Oct 92 **Myself** and the President met. Minister.

Nov 92 Coalition was **broke** up - Politician on "Prime Time".

Nov 92 Preparing for the hust**lings** - F.F. Politician.
He **thought** me everything I knew - General usage.

Oct 92 Poor **mis**fortunate people. - Presenter - Radio.

Jan 93 Mome**n**to presented on his achievement - Common.

Oct 92 So the weather is **downcast** is it then?- Radio presenter.

Dec 92 Late News will be at **Half-Eleven** - News Presenter.

Nov 92 I have **wrote** - Musician - T.V. News.

Dec 92 **Alternate** used for **alternative** - Radio presenter.
'**robbery** of money' - 1 p.m. News, Radio interviewer.
I must have **wrote** your name - musician.
whose hub-caps were **robbed** - Newspaper.
9 p.m. in the eveningtime; mild temperatures - Weather
presenter.

Nov 92 He pulled off a **defeat** - Ed. Newspaper.

Dec 92 People like **myself** and Andrew Morton - T.V.
Dick Spring is a man Irish people have **credibility** in.
- Labour T.D.

Dec 92 **Myself** and a group of nuns went in - Radio.

Dec 92 A coh**er**ent Party - Labour speaker in Parliament.

Dec 92 That's all from the Show for tonight, so till tomorrow
night, good **evening**! - Radio presenter.

Dec 92 V**oi**lent attack perpetrated - Gardai.
He was a member of the traffic **corpse** - Garda.

Nov 92 Everything was **robbed** out of his case - Radio 1 and others.

Dec 92 Poi**gn**ant (sounding the "g") - T.V. Common.
A politician **that** was active - T.V. presenter.
People **that** are used **of** it - General, rural.

Nov 92 There **was** seven murders in the North - Politician.

Oct 92 **Irregardless** of what I **done** ... on **myself** and John
He **done** his prayers every day - English teacher on L.L.S.

Oct 92 Mr. Haughey's evidence finished at 3.30 this **evening**
- Radio Reporter.

Oct 92 A child's first 5 years **effects** his future - Newspaper.

Nov 92 **Robbed** his car from the driveway - Radio 2 presenter.
Do you rob things - Radio.

1993 Prices are **dearer**; temperatures are **colder** - repeatedly on
R.T.E.
Not very different **than** - a common usage.

Mar 93 47 adults, 15 of whom were children - Spokesperson (on
Farming).
Trad**es** Union - Newspaper - (3 times).

Mar 93 **Myself** and ..... went - Guest on Radio show.

Mar 93 Vagaries pronounced **ve'gā-rees** - Radio presenter.

Apr 93 "Radio 1 Midnight News" reader finished with **"Good
Morning"** - no greeting at start. (was (s)he unsure?).

Apr 93 Some on R.T.E. say to audience: I'd like to "introduce **you to**"
(should be vice versa).

Mar 93 'You can make the **distinguishment** between sounds' - Radio
1 presenter.

Jan 93 We're never **took** aside and told we **done** well, - A caller to Radio 1 Show.

Jan 93 **Ourselves** and the Labour Party - Politician on Radio 1.

Jan 93 A doctor who **robbed** manuscripts from the Library - An ex-teacher, on Radio 1.

Jan 93 "Good Evening" at 2 p.m. -- A school principal on Radio 1.

Jan 93 You **only need** one - Radio advert.
Get a more **younger** type into the Party - Politician and teacher.
Loved **one** another, (when referring to **two** people) - Common
Theatre pronounced The-a͞a-ter - Common error.

June 93 He sank into a deep drain which was concealed by water - Radio 1 News 6.30 p.m.

June 93 No rift between **either** the Taoiseach or the Tánaiste - Newscaster, 9 p.m. T.V. News.

June 93 Armagh looked the more **hungrier** team - Oppos. Captain.
Dublin is a dangerous place to be - Radio presenter.
At **Half-nine** - R.T.E. programme signpost.
Confusion of **coherent** and **cohesive** - Common.
Also people phoning presenters on R.T.E. keep saying "how are you" over and over, and presenter keeps answering "not too bad" over and over, every 30 seconds, often.

Nov 93 Problems between **both** sides - T.V. presenter.
He was forced to **lay** down - Garda Superint. [Americanism].

Nov 93 **Myself** and Jim - Secondary teacher on Radio.
Cedric pronounced Se͞edrick - presenter on Radio 1.
What **bewaits** England (v All-Blacks) - T.V. Sports presenter.

Nov 93 Without **them** knowing it - Radio 1 presenter.

Dec 93 P.D.'s **advice** youth to get involved - Newspaper.
Disected piece by piece; stress on di - Common.

Dec 93 Heart-rendering: To progress (wrong accent - emphasis on first syllable) - Politician.

Dec 93 Niall Quinn is crocket; **themselves** and Everton - Newspaper.
Advertisements now say: **May** I help you?

Dec 93 I can look quite good-looking - caller on G.B.S.
Between **12** midnight and 8 a.m. **in the morning**.
Man on News.

Dec 93 Batten **up** your hatches - Gale forecaster.

Dec 93 Missed-interpretation - Politician in Dáil;
duz not **deteriate** - Minister.

Dec 93 **Thumps** up; **rarin** to go - Newspaper.

Dec 93 The future isn't **conducive** from any point of view to **me** saying anything - Politician.

Q. Do you **think** the Coalition will survive - reporter.
A. I **hope** so - politician (not the appropriate answer).

June 93 It's like going into a shop and **robbing** £1,000
Its not **in any difference** to tax evasion - Politician
(He started a sentence and didn't finish it, repeatedly)
- Common habit in Ireland.

June 93 They kicked **he** and his friends - 9 a.m. News Reporter.
F.F. and their bethroth-**ed** Labour. - "It Says in the Papers"
That's all from the programme, Good Morning - Radio Presenter.
Sore shoulder - commonly used for **painful** shoulder.

July 93 He took the safer **rout** to the green - T. V. presenter.

July 93 He was the **best** player on the day (2 players) - T.V. presenter on Becker v Sampras (tennis).

May 93 Courtesy (emphasis on Ō) - common everywhere
Dose tings; I wouldn't have **went**; **2 tousand udder tings has** to be done. **Dey** are; **De** score.
I was **dere** - **Tursday**. **Secetry** - Common errors.

May 93 Myself, John Giles and Eamonn Dunphy - T.V. programme.

May 93 Whether **or not** - 6.01 T.V. News presenter.
(This is a most common utterance everywhere).

June 93 R.T.E. News for the Deaf script on Trade Unions showed Unions with a small **u.**
What happened when you **both** met each other - Radio 1 presenter.
Workers **that** are threatened in Aer Lingus - Reporter.
Terribly generous - T.V. presenter.
Weatherman said "Goodnight" at start .
C.V.'s; Goff's etc. (apostrophes often superfluous).

June 93 The-**āā**-tre; you **can** get up now - T.V. presenter.
'You get tired shaking hands with the same oul faces' - Supporter on match.

June 93 Intervention beef was **robbed** - Radio presenter.

June 93 It was **terribly** funny, **terribly** good - Reporter on Radio 1.
Ect, ect; whether **or not** - Presenter on 6.01 News.
Himself and his classmates - Corres. 6.01 News.

July 93 But the E.E.C. were **only willing** to offer 7.5 billion - T.V. News presenter.

July 93 There was a **sink** in each bedroom - Radio writer.
Aren't I - Common enough in media.

July 93 On 5 p.m. Radio News, reader said "Good Evening". At 5.20 p.m. on same programme, reporter said: "Good Afternoon".

July 93 1.11 - read "One point eleven" on 6.01 News - Newsreader.
Drink your soup - T.V. programme.
If he **was** there, for Present Tense (that is Past Tense).

July 93 A Govt. Minister pronounced the word "Ministher". - T.V.
Gobnait - used as a man's name. - Radio.
Ad. on Radio: Brazil is a long way to go .
Irish tendency to pronounce French words as if they were English phonetically: **Jean** De Arc; Lourd**es,** Port **au Prince**' Tour De **France** etc.

July 93 Charges will be **pre**ferred - R.T.E. Radio 1.

Aug 93 The giraffes have 5 more offspring**s**, varying in heig**hth** - 6.01 T.V. News presenter.

Sept 93 Talks will be long, drawn out and protracted - T.V.

Dec 93 This is an histor**ical** document aimed towards peace between **both** traditions in Ireland - Politicians on News.
We're into a prize **mode** - Radio 1 presenter.
Dec 93 It came out **fantastic** - Author.

Sept 93 'Now that **voil**ence has ended in N.I. we must try to **secure** a **secure** settlement, no different **than** that achieved elsewhere, and involving **large numbers** of groups - Politician, Radio 1.

Oct 93 The people we've **went** to - Priest on G.B.S.
'**Ke**ltic v Rangers' - Radio presenter.

Oct 93 I feel sorry for Nuns who had to handle girls such as **I** - Writer (Guest) on T.V.

Oct 93 Liam Brady relaxes in Jury's **In** Hotel **Rarin'** to go - Newspapers.

Oct 93 With her **hands** crossed, so relaxed is she, jumping about like a jazelle - Ex-teacher.
Who was best, **him** or Pele? - T.V.

Oct 93 That **there will be** good sense prevail - Politician.

Oct 93 'Man City presented Terry Phelan with a **momentum**' - Newspaper.
Honey, I **shrunk** the Kids - Movie.

Dec 93 Obstacles remain between **both** sides - T. V. News.
He did it **terribly** well - Common error.
Curious - has it got two meanings?
Ye - old English plural, obsolete. Today - **You.**

Oct 93 If I **was** going to accept this criticism now, here - Politician in Dáil.

July 93 A **remarkable** person - does that mean "good" or "bad".

July 93 She is jumping **fantastic** - Horse Rider.
I have been **speaking with** - common nowadays.

July 93 **Herself** and her husband are now dead - Radio presenter.

July 93 Jacques Delors has a **sore** back - Radio presenter.
July 93 The weapon was as small as a **biro**
He **hung** his victim - Newspaper.

July 93 If I was a legal man, I'd be do**in terrible** well - Politician.

May 94 She worked there on **alternative** weeks - R.T.E. Radio presenter.

May 94 **Person**-made lake - Caller on Radio Show.

Nov 93 **Drinking** soup - Radio presenter.

Nov 93 Very heart-**rendering** indeed - Newspaper.

Nov 93 Sovereignity - Politician on Radio, 1.55 p.m.

Nov 93 D̄isect the posts - T.V. sports commentator.

Nov 93 Guilty of **robbing** the woman's handbag from the seat next to her, at the traffic lights - Radio presenter.

Nov 93 Cathal Casey had **began** well - Newspaper.

Nov 93 **Rarin** to go - Newspapers.

Nov 93 Believe it or **not**. Is this correct?

Dec 93 The more **stronger** teams - Radio 1 presenter.

Dec 93 On the **rout** between Dublin and London airports - Radio 1 Politician.

Dec 93 "Myself and my girlfriend" - a poet.

Dec 93 Nineteen Ninety **Tree** We'll lose compet-**iveness** - Politician.

Dec 93 Last night was **deadly**, really good - Radio 1.

Nov 93 They did nothing to **quell** the number of homeless
    - University Student.
    Phone: 424242 [Pron. Forty-Two, Forty-Two, Forty-Two]
A.   Pron. Four Two Four Two Four Two.
    [424242 is one complete number, not three 42's]
    Also 1.42 [Pron. One point **forty-two**]
A.   Pron. One point four two.
    [A decimal point figure is not a complete intact number]

Jan 94 Do you know anyone **that** - Advertisement.
    "Aren't I" - Letter 23/12/93 and 19/1/94 - Newspapers.

Jan 94 Baby, you **can't** touch my car - Advert on Radio.

Jan 94 Anyone **that** would think like that - Politician.

Jan 94   We treat our audience **terribly** well - T.V. presenter.

Jan 94   He played fairly **good** - Radio Sports presenter.

Jan 94   Its not only **him** who said it - Radio 1 presenter.

Jan 94   Had an **enterview** with him in **An**gland - (Common with
         people not sure of the language; or eager to impress).

Jan 94   'Octapus', '**Imm**igrate to America', 'ceders' - Newspaper.

Jan 94   The Minister is **winding** her way through it - 6.01 News.

Jan 94   Between Canada and **America**?! - R.T.E. T.V. programme.

Jan 94   I would have **went** in - Newspaper man on Radio 1.

Jan 94   No sooner had farmers **began** - Correspondent,
         6.01 T.V.

Jan 94   Christmas trees were **robbed** - Newspaper.

Jan 94   To be shown Tuesday

Feb 94   The price of houses is very **dear** - Radio presenter.

Feb 94   The Corporation collect the **refuge** every Monday - Common.

Feb 94   **There's** conflicting reports - 9 p.m. T.V. News.
Feb 94   We are holding the mungrel at this **point** in time - Gardaí.

Feb 94   There's a **weaver** system in operation for Water Charges -
         Politician.

Feb 94   When the Golding's lives are influenced
         Tsar Nicholas 11 (eleven) - Newspaper.
         Confusion of "Premier Division" and "First Division" in
         soccer.
         "Mathematics" for mere sums, should be **"Arithmetic"**.

Feb 94 What a wonderful place Limerick must be **to live**.
Crossword clue: 'Searches and **robs** from fliers' - Newspaper.

Feb 94 But **over**-passes it far too much
At the edge of **he's** area - Radio.

Feb 94 There **has** been various leaks - Politician.

Feb 94 Match being played in **J**erez (**j** pronounced) - Radio Sport.

Feb 94 Thank you for **speaking with** me - Radio presenter.

Feb 94 "If you want them to stop, don't start" - Advertisement.

Mar 94 Calling for the **outing** of the Minister from the Government
- Radio 1.

Mar 94 Announcer said: Sunday at **half-one**. Is that 12.30 or 1.30
[In Germany it is 12.30].

Mar 94 County Athlone - Contestant on T.V. quiz programme .
By Killarney's Lake's -Banner headline - Newspaper.

Mar 94 It is written in **biro** - Radio presenter.

Mar 94 Not being **thought** to do work.
She **never** heard such common sense in a **long time**
They hurt **theirselves** (a caller) - Radio programme.

Mar 94 I'll be back tomorrow, till then, enjoy the rest of the evening
- T.V. News.

Mar 94 It can't be **remediated** [Remedied]
- Politician and teacher.

Mar 94 You'll see **me** and Daniel Day Lewis - T.V.

Mar 94 Heloise (H sounded) - Radio 1.

Mar 94 A mixture of fear and **a mixture of** panic - Caller to Radio.

Mar 94 Judge, pronounced ŭ instead of as in Jodge. - Newspaper - Common in Connacht.

Apr 94 Not treat them any different **to** - Radio presenter.

Apr 94 **Robbery** of £15,000 - T.V. News.

Apr 94 People should make **up** their own decision - Radio guest.

Apr 94 12.30 p.m. 'Good Morning!' - Radio presenter to guest. (very common up to 1 p.m.).

Apr 94 Presenter said "Goodnight" at **start** of soccer match. Also Tilberg pron. **Teel**berg - T. V.

Apr 94 'Power to G.P.'s - script on T.V. programme.

Apr 94 Of the 12th **instance** - Radio presenter.

Apr 94 Teacher of English on Radio kept saying 'whether **or not**; ' also kept changing to another thought in mid-sentence.

Apr 94 There will be no more happ**ier** Minister - Radio 1.

Apr 94 **Mis**fortunate woman - Radio.

Apr 94 The **amount** of women **that** - Radio.

Apr 94 **Myself** and Gerry Ryan - Radio presenter. **Himself** and Paul Harrington celebrated - Radio presenter.

Apr 94 I will take that particular **rout** - Politician.

Apr 94 Thats all from the **"Morning** Programme" for this **morning,** so until tomorrow **morning,** good **morning!** - Radio 1.

May 94 He was fairly **shook** himself, **like, you know** - witness, on Radio.

May 94 One person said "Good Evening" at 5 p.m.
another correctly said "Good Afternoon" at 5 p.m. - Radio.

May 94 He be**trayed** the **voi**lence very well - caller, about a play.

May 94 Changed the **formality** of the programme - caller, Radio.

June 94 The position is un**tee**nable - Radio 1 caller.

July 94 Their trust had been **mis**betrayed - Radio News.
This phenom**ena**.

Aug 94 Bought at the **cheapest** of prices - Radio presenter.

On the Dublin to Galway **Rd.**
The baby is O.K., the **kids** mind **it** - Common.

Aug 94 In the **throes** of an economic boom - Newspaper.

Aug 94 Complem**ented** for his achievement - Newspaper.
(Common confusion between "complimented" and "complemented").

Aug 94 He was **unbelievable** (remarkable, amazing) - Common (Does that mean good or bad?).

Aug 94 From 9.30 a.m. in the morning till 9 p.m. at night - Advert.
the meeting between **both** sides lasted - Radio - Common

Aug 94 One boat was earth-**ed** on the bank (emphasis on **ed**).⎫
⎬ Same
Aug 94 The other was **berth-ed** at the jetty - Common.⎭

Aug 94 I have never **drank** - Politician.

Sept 94 The car hit a **three** in **Thrim**. 5 males are now deceased

- Garda spokesman on Radio.

Sept 94 We were **both** colleagues on the L.L. Show - Guest on Radio
programme.

Sept 94 On Radio 1, the Mayor of Coventry was asked what he
attributed his 'mayor-**ality**' to.
He thought it was **"morality"** and answered accordingly.
The Interviewer mispronounced **Mayoralty** [There is no **"i"**].

Apr 94 Opponents **to** the Mullaghmore project - Reporter on Radio
News.

Sept 94 I don't **talk** English out here - Teacher on Radio show.

Apr 94 There **are** a whole **series** of people - Politician, Radio 1.

Sept 94 Why not **lay** down and rest (americanism) - Newspaper.

Oct 94 Expensive **prices** at Goff's - 6.01 T.V.

Oct 94 'Linster House' - Radio 1 News.
(This is a Mayo-Connacht error).
The kids **seen** it and **done** it and are used **of it** - Common.

Mary Robinson

NOTES

One of the longest words in the English language:
> 'Antidisestablishmentarianism' (28 letters)

is really an amalgam of different words or parts: -
> Anti-dis-establishment-arian-ism.

A common utterance in schools is:-
> 'Please Sir (Miss) **can** I go to the toilet'?

A.   Please Sir (Miss) may I go to the toilet?

> ["Can I" means am I physically **able** to
> The meaning intended here is the **seeking** of **permission**
> = "May I"

> Stating the obvious, unnecessarily, is a common Irish practice
> e.g. (a) "kicking **foot**ball", (b) "8 a.m. **in the morning**" (c) This
> is the "Sunday Show".

A.   (a) it is **obvious** that a **foot**ball is for kicking, so correct way
is: "Playing football", or "kicking ball".
(b) 8 a.m. **means** "morning"; so say "8 a.m." or "8 in the
morning".
(c) "This is the Sunday Programme" - it can hardly be
otherwise if the day is Sunday.

N.B.   This rule could even apply to names on guesthouses. If the
house is **obviously** overlooking the sea, there is no great
imagination or originality in calling the house "Sea View".

> Confusion of "s" and "z" sounds (and sometimes "c")[*1]
> e.g. "excuses" and excuzes; disown (dizown)
> [*1] decision (dezizion).

A.   The "z" sound is often mis-used for "s" and for "c".

> 'Are **ye** going to the pub'   *'Half-eleven' could be 11/2 = 5.5;*

A.   "Ye" is the archaic usage of   *or half of the hour of 11 = 10.30 as*
the modern plural "you".   *it does in Germany etc.*
"Ye" is used mainly in rural areas.

The terms "lady" and "gentlemen" are today loosely applied
to every "woman" and "man". Recently a criminal was

referred to as 'the gentleman in custody'. Traditionally these terms were reserved for persons of proven worthiness; of grace, breeding, manners etc. The terms should not mean merely "male" or "female" but their application should be earned and deserved.

I **seen** that; I **done** that
These are probably the most common "errors" in everyday Irish speech.

A.   I **saw** that; I **did** that [Past Tense].
The correct usage for "seen" and "done" is:
I **have seen** that; I **have done** that [Past Participle].

He bought it **off** me.
A.   He bought it from me.

The player is suffering from a hamstring ————
He had a medical ————
A.   The player is suffering from a hamstring **injury.**
He had a medical **examination.**
The sense of the above examples is incomplete
a "hamstring" is not an injury
a "medical" is not an examination.

His **hand** was injured at the elbow.
A.   His **arm** was injured at the elbow.
[The hand is the 8" extremity, with fingers].

Down won the All-Ireland ————
A.   Down won the All-Ireland **title.**
(Same incomplete sense as above).

A **pair** of scissors; a **pair** of trousers.
A.   A scissors;   trousers.
[There can't be one scissor; it takes two **blades** to make **one** scissors]. No need to say "pair".

He wore a **pair** of swimming togs.
A.   He wore [   ] swimming togs.
[One person cannot wear **two** togs(i.e. pair)

"Togs" implies **one** unit, (with two leg-openings)].

She owns a hairdressing **saloon.**
She owns a hairdressing salon [French].

A.   A common error
[The root of both words is the same = large room
but nowadays they have developed separate meanings].

It has long been observed that women are better speakers, readers, linguists and conversationalists than men.

Scientists have now demonstrated this graphically, showing women's brains to have a larger speech area.

It is fortunate then, and not just for their gentle, caring, and loving qualities, that most teachers of the young are women, as children need "models" in communication training.

Evidence of the excellence of women speakers in Irish public life is to be had, even without selection, in probably the very first three who come to mind, viz.: President Mary Robinson; Professor Mary McAleese; and Mary Harney M.P. (T.D.), the latter whose verbal brilliance was witnessed on nationwide T.V. coverage of Parliament (Dáil) during the Government fall in November - December 1994. Added to this is the exquisite articulation and eloquent delivery of R.T.E. news - reader Ann Doyle, and others.

Mary Harney, T.D.

CHAPTER 3
CORRECTIONS

In the lists given here, it is not to be implied that these are 'errors' in English, objectively, finally and without question. What is given here are the subjective **opinions** of the author, not a definitive, immutable law. The 'errors' in speech and script are those **perceived** to be so by the author, who, being human, is not without error himself, [despite being a teacher of English].

Furthermore, as the "errors" were observed in the main, in live speech situations on radio, T.V. and from politicians, it must be allowed that the pressures of media presentation might have influenced the speakers into hasty or unpremeditated utterances, thus exaggerating the propensity for error. Anyway, a speaker is usually repeating the speech pattern of his locality, county, province or country, so the "fault" is often a cultural, collective or educational idiosyncracy.

Indeed, the purpose of this book is to address the question of "Irish English" on a national and educational level, and not on a personal or individual or celebrity basis. The individual references are unavoidable since that is the only way we can hear or clearly decipher speech. But it is the collective corpus of all of these individuals that gives the total, national picture in regard to the state of the language, 'as she do be spoke, like, y'know'.

The drizzle will become **more patchier.**

A. This should read:- will become **patchier.**
or:- will become **more patchy.**

Instead of **us** doing it.

A. Instead of **our** doing it.

Poor **mis**fortunate people.

A. Poor, **un**fortunate people.

[No such word as "misfortunate". "Misfortune" is a noun and cannot be used as an adjective, in the above construction.]

Myself and the President spoke ...

A. The President and I (myself) spoke

["Myself" is a synonym of or the apposite of "I". It is wrong to say: 'Myself spoke']

33

(a) It is incorrect to say 'myself .... spoke'
(b) It is bad manners to put one-self first.

He was given a **momento** of his visit.

A.   He was given a memento of his visit.

The weather is **downcast** today.

A.   The weather is overcast today.

Had I not **went**.

A.   Had I not **gone**.

Irregardless of what I do (Double negative).

A.   Regardless of what I do.
["Ir" and "Less" are both opposite in meaning to "regard"
here; :: two negatives = positive = Regard.
No such word as "irregardless"].

Mr. Haughey's evidence finished at 3.30 this **evening**

A.   Evening doesn't start till 6 p.m. :: 3.30 this **afternoon**.

Arsenal **sunk** Nottingham Forest.

A.   Arsenal sank Nottingham Forest (Past Tense).
or Nottingham Forest **were sunk** by Arsenal (Past Participle).

Q.   Poignant.
A.   The "g" is silent, as in "sign". [Poyn-yant]

A child's first 5 years **effects** his future.

A.   A child's first 5 years **affects** his future.
[Effect: carry out.   Affect = influence]

I have **wrote** several songs.

A.   I have written several songs.
[Wrote = past tense; have written = past participle]

He pulled off a **defeat**.

A.   "Pulled off" means success or a win, not a defeat.

Francis Fitzgerald gave her opinion.

A.   Frances Fitzgerald gave her opinion. [Francis - man].

He was **rarin'** to go (common misprint in papers).

A.   He was **rearin'** to go (equine).
[This comes from a horse **rearing** up on his hind legs, in his eagerness to go].

He **robbed** £1,000. The car's hub-caps were **robbed**.

A.   He stole £1,000. The car's hub-caps were stolen.
[Rob = to steal from = He "**stole from**" £1,000 - wrong
As the £1,000 had no money on it, it could not be "robbed", same for the hub-caps.]

He wished to **disassociate** himself from those remarks.

A.   He wished to **dissociate** himself from those remarks.
[Disassociate presumes a **prior** association, ∴ its meaning is not the one **usually** intended.
It is correct, however, if meant, literally].

Often times.   A. Often or many times.
[Often times is archaic = oft-times]

Divide regions between **each other.**

A.   Divide regions between them (selves) (plural).
["Each other" is singular = one person.
You cannot divide things between **one** person].

Having my hand **shook.**

A.   Having my hand shaken.

We are a united, **coherent** political **party.**

A.   We are a united, cohesive political Party.
[A particular or proper noun must have a capital letter, i.e. Party]. ["Coherent" and "Cohesive" often confused].

Two **complementary** tickets.
Two **complimentary** tickets [common error].

A. We will take a different **route** (pronounced **rout**)
We will take a different route (pronounced rōot).

The time is **half-eleven.**
A. The time is half past eleven.

Alternate and **Alternative** often confused for each other or accepted as synonymous words.
But they have different and separate meanings.

Soccer - Speak: (Cliches)
Hoped to get a **result**, but were beaten 3-2.
The odd goal in 3.
Goalie given no chance.
Ref. had no hesitation.
Dropped from the **Premier** to the **First** Division.
[But "Premier" means "First"].

9 p.m. in the evening-**time** (archaic, poetic).
A. 9 in the evening.
[Actually "9 p.m." is sufficient on its own, as it is obvious that 9 p.m. is evening].

Giving us **mild** or **cool** temperatures.
A. Temperatures are rates or degrees of heat, ie. numbers, not qualities like **cool** or **warm.**
:: the correct statement is" "**mild** or **cool** weather".

Dick Spring is a man the Irish have **credibility** in.
A. Dick Spring is a man the Irish have belief in.
or to use the same word in its proper sense:
"To the Irish, Dick Spring is a man of credibility".

Prices are **dearer** in Galway (referring to houses).
A. It is the house that's dear, not the price.
The "price", like "temperature" above is "higher" or "lower" only.

Not very different **than** (or to).

A.   Not very different from.
      ["From" is the modern usage. "Than" is an "americanism" and
      both "than" and "to" are somewhat archaic].

      47 adults, 15 of them children.
A.   47 people, 15 of them children.
      [Or 32 adults and 15 children.]

      Trades Union.
A.   This term has become confused with Trade-Unions
      nowadays. If, as is usual, the plural of Trade-Union is
      intended, then the latter is correct. "Trades Union" means a
      collection of Trades, not the intended collection of Unions.

      Crulety (crew-let-ēe)
A.   Common mis-spelling and mispronunciation of Cruelty,
      properly pronounced "Crew-l-tee" or "crew-l-ti".

      The Bank **only** opens on weekdays.
A.   The bank opens only on weekdays [or: on weekdays only].

      Inestēēmable
A.   Improper pronunciation of "Inestimable" [In-es-tim, ebll].

      America and Canada.
A.   The continent of North America contains Canada, so
      properly, "The United States and Canada".

      Incidenc**es** or Incident**ences**
A.   Common confusion here between "incidents", "incidence" and
      "instances". All three have different meanings and there are
      no such words as "Incidenc**es**" or "Incident**ences**".

      Ec Cetera (**ect.**) (Common mispronunciation).
A.   Et Cetera (etc.)

      The Coalition was **broke** up; it wasn't our fault.
A.   The Coalition was broken up; it wasn't our fault.

Preparing for the hustlings.
A.   Preparing for the hustings.

He **thought** me everything I know about Fianna Fáil.
A.   He taught me everything I know about Fianna Fáil.

Thats all from the .... Show for **tonight**, so until tomorrow
night, good **evening**!
A.   (a) Too long-winded and repetitive ("night").
(b) "Good evening"should not follow "night" (jarring).
(c) "Good evening" usually means "hello" for as "Goodbye" or
"Goodnight" is intended here.
A.   Thats all for tonight, so until tomorrow, goodbye.

We in the Gardaí would see it as a **voilent** attack.
A.   We in the Gardaí would see it as a violent attack.

The Garda Traffic **Corpse** were alerted.
A.   The Garda Traffic Corps (pron. **Cōre**) [French].

A politician **that** was active, in F.F.
A.   A politician who was active, in F.F.
["who" is a **personal** pronoun, for as "that" refers to **common**
nouns or inanimate objects].

Charges will be **preferred** against him.
A.   Charges will be proffered against him.

Make the **distinguishment** between them.
A.   Make the distinction between them.
[No such word as the former].

We're never **took** aside and told we **done** well.
A.   We're never taken aside and told we did well.

Ourselves and Labour are a good Coalition, in 1994.
A.   Labour and we (ourselves) are a good Coalition, in 1994.
[Never put yourself first, in etiquette or elocution].

(a) He **robbed** priceless manuscripts from the Chester Beatty Library.

(b) All of her valuables were **robbed** from her bag.

A.   Stolen. This common error is repeated again and again.

Good **Evening**, welcome to the programme, its 2 p.m.

A.   Good Afternoon, welcome to the programme, its 2 p.m. [Evening begins at 6 p.m.]

(a) We need a more **younger** type in the Party.

A.   We need a more young type in the Party.

(b) Armagh looked a more **hungrier** team.

A.   Armagh looks a more hungry team.

The two people loved **one another.**

A.   For two people only, it is **each other.**
one another - more than two.

Theatre - commonly mispronounced Thea-a̅a-ther.

A.   Theatre (pron. Theater, Theeeter) - one vowel.

No rift between **either** the Tánaiste or the Taoiseach.

A.   "Either" denotes singular number, i.e. one person, not two.
:: there cannot be a rift between a person, between one.
Delete "either" for correct sense.

No rift between her (President) and the Government.

A.   No rift between the Government and her (Objective case).

Dublin is a dangerous place to be ...... [unfinished]

A.   "To be" on its own is Intransitive and does not denote place. Correct sense is 'to be **in** ' [Transitive Verb]. or "**in** which to be".

Put your friendship aside for a **split second** and tell us all.

A.   Put your friendship aside for "a little while" and tell us all. "Split second" is an obvious exaggeration in conversation time.

39

They are coming off the field with their heads **between their legs.**

A.   They are coming off the field with their heads down. [Tails].
Another obvious exaggeration (and physical impossibility).

The Government are willing to hold a referen**da**

A.   A referendum. Referenda is plural (Latin grammar).

He was a man of **amazing** cunning**ness.**

A.   He was a man of great cunning.

He was **amazing, unbelievable,** absolutely **remarkable.**

A.   These adjectives do not adequately qualify the noun; we still do not know if "he" was amazingly good or amazingly bad. [Florid, exaggerated language].

He scored a most **fortuitous** goal, as time was up.

A.   He scored a most fortunate goal, as time was up.
More correctly: 'he was fortunate to score'.
[Fortuitous means "by chance", not the intended meaning
Fortunate means lucky, the intended inference here].

Inter**est**ed (often pronounced "Inter-**rest**-edd")

A.   Inter**est**ed. (pron. Intrested) with no stress on the middle syllable **"res"**, but on the first, **Int.**

(T.V.) Now, ladies and gentlemen (audience), I'd like to introduce **you to** .....

A.   Now, ladies and gentlemen (audience), I'd like to introduce to you.....
[The guest (performer) is the one being introduced, not the audience, who are a greater number and already there].

Schedule (pron. Skedule).

A.   This is an "americanism".
The English/European pron. is **"Shedule"**.

He gradually got **used of it.**

A.   He gradually got used to it.

We in Fianna Fáil will seek to **mitigate** against this.

A.   We in Fianna Fáil will seek to militate against this,
or mitigate this. Confusion of words here.

It is not .... in any difference ... **to** tax evasion.

A.   There is confusion of thought and speech here.
The speaker changes tack in mid-sentence, twice.
What the Minister was trying to say was:
'It is the same as tax evasion'
or 'It is no different from tax evasion'
[Not finishing sentences is a common practice here].

They kicked **he** and his friend on the ground.

A.   They kicked **him.**
This is a sentence, subject (they), verb ("kicked"), object (him).
:: "Him" is Objective Case; "he" can only be Subjective.

Dislocated shoulder, very **sore.**

A.   Dislocated shoulder, very painful.
["Sore" refers to superficial irritants, e.g. sore skin or cut.
Injuries to bones are referred to as "painful" or "aching"].

In gineral, he always attends Linster House.

A.   In general, he always attends Leinster House.
[This habit applies especially in Connacht] [Mayo].

His **noo** book sold a **millen** copies, **dat's** good.

A.   His new book sold a million copies, thats good.
[This habit applies especially in Munster].

The safer **rout** to the green (rout).

A.   The safer route (ro͞ot) to the green.

Line-outs (Lines-out), Attorney-generals (Attorneys-general)

A.   A recent trend tends to go for "Lines-Out" and Attorneys-
general, but the meaning is lost or distorted thereby: "Line-
outs" obviously refers to rugby, for as "Lines-Out" is vague
and ambiguous. Normally a hyphenated word is understood

to be one word, e.g. Lineout, of which the plural is "Lineouts" or "Line'outs".
[I believe that the original is correct].

On the day he was the **best** player of the two.
A.   On the day he was the better player of the two.
"Better" is a comparative between **two** only.
"Best" is a superlative/absolute, and singular, meaning "pick of the pack" or "top of the group".

Courtesy, properly pron. "curtesy" today
[but many Irish people retain the literal, middle-English pron. from **Court** (kort) i.e. "Kōrtesy" or "Cōrtesy"].

Tousands of dose **tings has** to be done **dere** on de Tursday.
A.   Thousands of those things have to be done there on (the) Thursday.
[Common errors nationwide in **Republic**, especially in Dublin and Cork].

Whether or **not** he knew / or whether he knew **or not**
A.   Whether he knew ["whether" implies either/or, one or the other, so there is no need to add "or not", it is already implied].

You **can't** smoke between **half-one** and **half-six**
A.   You may not smoke between half past one and half past six or 1.30 - 6.30.
[**Can't** refers to "ability to"
N.B. "May not" refers to "permission to" - the meaning intended here
"Half-six" could be 6/2 = 3 or 1/2 of the hour of 6 = 5.30.
"Half-six" in Germany **is** 5.30; so the term is unclear].

He could **only pick** one winner.
A.   He could pick only one winner.

Will I bring in your tea now, madam?
A.   Shall I bring in your tea now, madam?

[Interrogative case, i.e. a question = shall I?]

I shall! I will! I mean it!

A.   "I shall" means **intention**, "I intend to".

"I will" means **determination to**, e.g. "I will, I warn you".

*[1]   I **tok** the **bok** to **lok** to see if I had **pot** my **fot** in it.

A.   I took the book to look .... put my foot in it.

(tuk) (buk) (luk) (put) (fut).

[This is the snob language of those who may think "brok"

(Buk) sounds "common" and must be an error. They may

think that "**bok**", being posh, must therefore be right.

(Affected speech of some people)].

He was charged with **robbing** antiques and metals.

A.   Impossible! Antiques and metals don't carry money or goods.

The appropriate word is "**stealing**"

[Rob = "steal from", not "steal"]

I was the one, who was nominated **tuh**[1] ring.

I **rung**[2] **two times**[3]. **Charless**[4] Haughey was not involved.

Any person could have **rang**[5].

[Political newspeak].

A.   I was ...... **to**[1] .... **rang**[2] **twice**[3]. **Charles**[4] .... **rung**[5].

[N.B. Charles (one syllable) is occasionally given two

syllables, wrongly, in rural areas, e.g. "Char-less"].

*[1]   It is for **wemen** to make such a **dezision**.

A.   It is for women to make such a decision.

[*[1] This is similar to the "snob" language above or of someone

unsure of his language].

Princess Anne's paternity **suite** (sweet) v Mark Phillips.

A.   Princess Anne's paternity suit v Mark Phillips.

[**Suite** = furniture. Suit = lawsuit].

"Mary and I". "Mary and me"?

A.   ["Mary and I" is correct in **Subjective Case**; the subject.

"Mary and me" is correct in **Objective Case**; the object of the sentence.

It wasn't **us** in F.F. who put pressure on them.

A.   It wasn't we in F.F. who put pressure on them.
[Despite the widespread common use, **"us"** is incorrect as **Subject "Us"** is always in the Objective Case].

The **perceptive** that F.F. are responsible for Semi-State scandals.

A.   The perception that F.F. are responsible for Semi-State scandals.
["Perceptive" is an adjective, ∴ incorrect usage here].

The **Secetry** of the Dept. said the estimates had **overran**.

A.   The Secretary of the Dept. said the estimates had over-run.
[Secretary - from **secret**. "had" before "ran" makes it "run" as it changes **Past Tense** to **Past Participle**].

How about this one **either**? (Common in Leitrim etc.)

A.   How about this one also (or: as well).

In the **centre** of the bed.

A.   In the middle of the bed.
["Centre" us. refers to a circle, ring or sphere, usually with all equal points of radius].

De udder fella was very **umorous**. **Dey** all said **dat.**

A.   The other fella was very humorous. They all said that.
[De, Dat, Dese, Dose: Common error in Southern Ireland, East and South]. The "h" in humorous must be sounded.

I made the **ultimate sacrifice** for Fianna Fáil.

A.   ["ultimate sacrifice" is generally taken to mean death (martyr)]. [Who said dead men don't speak!!]

The jŭdge showed he was **inter-rest-ed**

A.   The judge (jodge) showed he was interested (Intrsted).
[In Connacht judge is often pron. soft "u"].

	He will **rise** the castle again, on the same site.
A.	He will raise the castle, again, on the same site.

	José Carreras **sung** beautifully.
A.	[J in Spanish pronounced **H**. "Sang" is the correct Past Tense.
A.	(José Carreras sang beautifully).

	'**Holloween** goodies
A.	Halloween goodies.

[From old English: All **Hallows** Eve (Evening) meaning: All Saints].

	The **san dōons** in Portmarnock.
A.	The sand dunes in Portmarnock.

["Dōon" sound, is an "americanism"].

	There are **less** wild men here in Trinity now.
A.	There are fewer wild men here in Trinity now.

["less" refers to non-human, inanimate objects].

	The bishop had no objection to **me** coming here.
A.	The bishop had no objection to my coming here.

	But I can't read **Peruvian** (no such language, unless ancient Inca).
A.	But I can't read Spanish.

	He **seen** the Kremlin while he **done** a tour of Moscow.
A.	He saw the Kremlin while he did a tour of Moscow.

["I seen", "I done", the two most common errors in Irish English].

	He **disected** the fairway.
A.	He bisected the fairway. [Bisect = cut in two].

[A common error. No such word as "disect" (an americanism) Apparent confusion between **"disect"** and **bisect** and **dissect**].

Q.	Do you mean to say that you were not there at all?
A.	No. I wasn't there. I was not there at all.

[Confusion of **sense** here. The answer should be **Yes!** as the
Q. was: "do you mean to say"? and not: "were you there"?]

The **richesness** of Joyce is familiar to us politicians.

A. [Confusion of thoughts and words here.
Confusion of "riches" and "richness", either would do here].

A great **tril**, and all for **tree** pounds.

A. A great thrill and all for three pounds.
[The old "**th**" problem, common in the Republic.
The opposite is the case in the North, where "tree" becomes
"three"].

She was **terribly** nice, **fierce** nice altogether.

A. [A contradiction: "terrible" and "fierce" are opposite to "nice"].

It can only be successful **but** on a **thrust** basis.

A. It can only be successful (but) on a trust basis.
or: It can be successful onlyon a trust basis.
["but" is superfluous and alters the intended sense].

You know what I mean, **like; you know,** like.

A. [Common practice: No known cure.
You know what I mean?]

Where is the **bathroom** in this restaurant, please.

A. [This is an "americanism" What is really required is a toilet or
lavatory] [No bathrooms in restaurants].

Basically, I am at college.

A. ['basically" is so overused that it has become a "cliche"].
A. I am at college.

He was very **curious** (ambiguous).

A. [Curious = odd, and also inquisitive].
[I would say: "He was very inquisitive" if I mean "enquiring"].

Ec Cetera (Ect.). Correction: Et Cetera (Etc.)
The oyster slipped straight down my **neck,** one gulp!

A. The oyster slipped straight down my throat, one gulp!
    [Some people regard **neck** and **throat** as the same thing,
    but neck is the external part only, throat = internal].

    I have a sore throath (also **troath**)
A. I have a sore throat.

    The **Residence** Association held their meeting.
A. The Residents Association held their meeting.
    [Residence = house' [Residents = People].

    He was accused of **fermenting** violence.
A. He was accused of fomenting violence (more usual)
    [Fermenting, e.g. grapes turning to wine etc.
    means "exciting" or stirring, both not usually with "violence"
    as in "fomenting"].

    I was **after** just **having went** out to the cow byre.
A. I had just gone out to the cow byre.
    ["I was after" is not standard English, but a direct translation
    of the Irish, Gaelic: "Bhí mé **tar éis** dul amach"].

    He put his **hands** around her and kissed her.
A. He put his arms around her and kissed her.
    [Hands are only about 8" long and couldn't surround a body].
    Some country men are ashamed to say "arms" because they
    have to sound "posh" and say "**awrms**', so instead they say
    "**ah-rums**" or "hands".

    Nobody came **anear** him (Archaic, Poetic).
A. Nobody came near him.

Proper Nouns (i.e. names of persons or things) always have capital
letters, e.g. Patrick, Elec. Trade Union.

    What happened when you **both** met?
A. What happened when you (two) met?
    ["Both" is superfluous and incorrect, logically, here; because
    it is obvious that **one** person cannot meet. "Both" is used to

stress or **emphasize two** as opposed to **one**, ∴ superfluous in this context of obvious meaning'].
"Two" is not necessary, if hearer/reader already knows.

He was **terribly** generous and **awfully** nice.

A.   He was very generous and very nice.
["Awful" archaic form = full of awe or wonder or fear or dread. "Terrible" archaic form = to terrify.
Today they are synonymous and have come to mean **"bad"** so in the above sentence they contradict "generous" and "nice".

C.V.'s; The Goff's; V.I.P.'s. The Whelan's.

A.   (1) The apostrophe is not appropriate if possession or ownership (possessive case) is not implied, or is singular.
(2) There can be no apostrophe inside in the case of **plural** number.
(3) If the **possessive** case, with **plural** number intended then the apostrophe goes outside the plural word:- e.g. Goffs' goods; the V.I.P.s' visas; The Whelans' neighbours.

It was given to **himself** and his classmates.

A.   It was given to his classmates and him(self).
(put self last - good manners and grammar).

Secetry - (common usage, vocally, in Ireland)

A.   Secretary (from 'secret')

The E.E.C. were **only** willing to offer Ireland £7.5 billion.

A.   The E.E.C. were (   ) willing to offer Ireland only £7.5 billion.
[The above sense "only willing" is wrong, as "only" qualifies "willing", whereas the intention is to qualify "£7.5 billion"].

There was a **sink** in each bedroom.

A.   There was a wash-basin in each bedroom.
[Polite speech says "basin"; sink = rough, kitchen etc.].
Aren't I.

A.   Amn't I [(Am I not, Am not I); incorrect to say "**Are** I not" [singular number]].

1.12 pron. one point twelve.

A.   One point one two.   .12 is not twelve, which is a whole figure.

Holloween, a mispronunciation of Halloween.
[From All Hallows (Saints) Eve or Evening]. [Repeat].

Drink your soup.

A.   Eat your soup. [Soup is not a drink].

If there **was** to be any deal done, it must be now.

A.   If there were to be any deal done, it must be now.
[Present Tense].

Brazil is a long way to go _____

A.   Brazil is a long way to go to
[or properly: Brazil is a long way to which to go].

Tour De **France**; Port Au **Prince**; **Jean** D'Arc, Lour**des**

A.   These are French, not English names and must be
pronounced in French i.e., Frawnce, Prawnce, Zhan, Loord.
[Common exception: Paris (Paree)].

Ye are all good players.

A.   You are all good players. [Ye = Archaic English]
[Properly: All of you are good players]
[In rural Ireland "Ye" survives as the plural of "You"].

Facination, mis-spelling of Fascination. Common.

She is jumping **fantastic**.

A.   She is jumping fantastically (properly: "very well").
[As it modifies the verb "jumping" it must be an adverb, for as
"fantastic" is an adjective and incorrect].

I have been **speaking with** Doris.

A.   I have been talking to Doris.
["Speaking with" is a modern term, and an "americanism"
It is ambiguous because "speaking with" could refer to two

strangers **separately** addressing a meeting, not each other, whereas the intention/meaning here is obviously a friendly chat **between** two (or more) people i.e. talk].

As small as a **biro.**
A.   As small as a ball-point pen.
[Biro is merely the inventor's name, not the pen itself].

He **hung** his victim.
A.   He hanged his victim.
["Hanged", though archaic, still is retained in the case of execution].

If I **was** a legal man (instead of a T.D.) I'd be doin' **terrible** well.
A.   If I were a legal man I'd be doing **very** well/or "terribly well".
[Terrible = Terror = bad = a contradiction of "well"
can't be "terrible" and "well" at the same time].

She worked there on **alternative** weeks.
A.   She worked there on alternate weeks.
[These two words are often confused, but are different].

Pollaphuca is a **person**-made lake.
A.   Pollaphuca is a **man**-made lake.
[In the modern rush to be "politically correct", "man" is now being used almost exclusively as being "male". But "Man" is a generic term for "humans" or "human race" and is still perfectly valid. "**A man**" refers to male].

They have five offsprings
A.   They have five offspring [The word is both singular and plural].

Themselves and their teacher went to the Zoo.
A.   Their teacher and they (themselves) went to the Zoo.
Talks will be **long, drawn out** and **protracted.**
A.   Talks will be (   ) protracted.
[These three adjectives are synonyms, they have the same

meaning, so **one** word suffices].

This is an histor**ic**al document between **both** traditions in Ireland.
A.   This is an historic document between the two traditions in Ireland.
[Historic (momentous, important) is the meaning relevant here. "Both" is emphazising a contrast with "one", and it is already obvious that you can't have an agreement between **one**]. Historical = relating to history.

We're in a prize-giving **mode** today.
A.   We're in a prize-giving mood today.
["Mode" is a new "americanism" being used in the wrong context. **Mode** is a "way of doing", while **mood** is "a feeling"].

It came out **fantastic**
A.   It came out really well or very well (or fantastically).
["Fantastic" is a verbose and emotive term, given to exaggeration].

V**oi**lence (common usage in Dublin city) [Pron. "Voy"].
A.   Vi**ol**ence [Pron. Vi].

Try to **secure** a **secure** settlement.
A.   Try to achieve a secure settlement.
[Repeating the same word unnecessarily is "bad taste"].
or
Thats all from "Today **Tonight**" for **tonight**, so until tomorrow **night**, good**night.**
A.   Same as above example, "night" repeated ad nauseum.

The people we priests have **went** to
A.   The people to whom we have gone (have gone to).

I feel sorry for nuns who had to handle girls such as **I.**
A.   I feel sorry for nuns who had to handle girls such as **me.**
[I = Subjective Case; **Me** = Objective Case, as applies here].

Jury's **In**

A.   Jury's Inn.

Jumping about like a **'jazelle"** (phonetic pronunciation)

A.   Jumping about like a gazelle

Who was **best, him** or Pele?

A.   Who was better, Pele or he? (Subjective case)
[In a comparison between only **two** people, "better" applies.
"best" = more than two]. "Best" is not comparitive.

As a F.F. Minister, I would like to see that **there will be good
sense prevail.**

A.   - that good sense will prevail.

Terry Phelan was presented with a **momentum** by Man. City.

A.   Terry Phelan was presented with a mememto by Man. City.

"Honey, I **shrunk** the **kids**" [Film]

A.   "Honey, I shrank the children". [or I've shrunk the children].
["Americanisms" again. Kids refers to young goats].

Obstacles remain between **both** sides.

A.   Obstacles remain between the sides.
[Same as examples given above'
[No need to say "both", as there can't be obstacles between
one side]. [Repeat].

If I as Taoiseach **was** going to accept this criticism now.

A.   If I as Taoiseach were going to accept this criticism now.
[Present Tense. Was = Past Tense].

He was **drinking** soup.

A.   He was eating soup. [Repeat].

It was very heart-**rendering.**

A.   It was very heart-rending.

Sovereign-**i**-ty

A.   Sovereignty (There is no second "i" or vowel)
[Pron. "Soverenty" almost as one syllable].

Di̅sects the posts (now in common use)

A.   Bisects the posts (There is no such word as **Disect**
"an americanism" and "dissects" means surgical cutting).

Cathal Casey had beg**an** well.

A.   Cathal Casey had begun well.

He was forced to **lay** down on the ground.

A.   He was forced to lie down on the ground.
[Americanism]

What **be**waits England?

A.   What awaits England?

Without **them** knowing it.

A.   Without their knowing it.

P.Ds. **advice** youth to get involved [Noun]

A.   P.Ds. advise youth to get involved [Verb, correct].

(a) To **pro**gress (Verb)   (b) He made **pro**gress [Noun]

A.   (a) To progress   (b) He made progress
[In (a) the stress should be on the second syllable **ress**
In (b) the stress should be on the first syllable **prog**].

If you don't mind **me** saying so.

A.   If you don't mind my saying so.

May I help you. (newly arrived form)

A.   Can I help you.
["May I" is arrogant and presumptious, he takes for granted
that he **can** help. "Can I" is more modest].

I can **look** quite good-**looking**.

A.   I can be quite good-looking [Repetition].

Between 12 **midnight** and 8 a.m. **in the morning.**

A.   Between midnight and 8 a.m.
["12" and "in the morning" are superfluous, because
"midnight" already implies "12 o'clock" and
8 a.m. = morning].

Batten **up** your hatches, its a real storm.

A.   Batten down the hatches (usually).

Thats a **missed**-interpretation and **duz** not reflect my Dáil
speech.

A.   Thats a misinterpretation and does not reflect my Dáil
speech.
[Phonetically, that is how it sounded to the listener].

If it **deteriates** further, I, as Minister will have to act.

A.   If it deteriorates further, I, as Minister will have to act.
[Common error].

The future isnt **conducive** to **me** saying anything.

A.   [An example of political "newspeak"]. No sense to it.

The more **stronger** teams prevail.

A.   The more strong teams prevail or: the stronger teams prevail
["Stronger" and "more strong" are comparative terms, to put
both together as above is a double comparative and is
:: superfluous and unnecessary and jarring].

The **rout** between Dublin and London airports {Rowt}

A.   The route between Dublin and London airports [Root]

Unless I as Minister act, the Nineteen Ninety **Tree** figures
show that we'll lose comp**eti**veness.

A.   Nineteen Ninety **Three** .... lose competitiveness
[Many people, Dubliners especially, do not pronounce **"th"**].

Last night was **deadly, brilliant!**
A.   Deadly means "bad". Brilliant here is slang for "good".
Both words are being used in the wrong context and are
opposites.

Did nothing to **quell** the number of homeless.
A.   Did nothing to reduce the number of homeless.

"Baby, you **can't** touch my car" - Advertisement.
A.   "Baby, you may not touch my car".
["Can't" implies physical inability] [May not = permission].

We treat our audience **terribly** well.
A.   We treat our audience exceptionally well.
["Terrible" and "well" are mutually exclusive].

He played fairly **good.**
A.   He played fairly well.
[To modify the verb "played" an adverb ("well") is needed
"good" is an adjective or/and a noun].

The Kennedys **immi**grated from Ireland.
A.   The Kennedys emigrated from Ireland.
[Emi = out; imm = in].

Un-earth-**ed** (phonetically) - common error in Ireland.
The last vowel "e" should not be stressed.
The word should be uttered in only **two** syllables: **Un-earthd**
not three as above. the last "e" should be silent.

The Minister is **winding** her way through it.
A.   The Minister is wending her way through it.

No sooner had farmers **began** [Past Tense].
A.   No sooner had farmers begun [Past Participle].

Hundreds of Christmas trees **robbed** from forestries.
A.   Hundreds of Christmas trees stolen from forestries.

[Christmas trees don't carry money, so cannot be robbed].

To be shown ___ Tuesday, morning **through** afternoon.

A.   To be shown on Tuesday, morning till afternoon.

[This is "american lingo", newly arrived here].

The price of houses is very **dear**

A.   The price of houses is very high.

[Prices are rates, either high or low] [It is the house that is dear, not the price]. [Repeat].

Ha-**rass** (emphasis on second vowel and syllable)

A.   Har'ass (emphasis on first vowel and syllable) [Harés]

[Ha-**rass** is an americanism, now widely used here so both are now acceptable].

All the **entrances** in the Round Ireland Race.

A.   All the entrants in the Round Ireland Race.

City **thēe-ātre** not effected.

A.   City theatre not affected. (one syllable in theatre)

[effect = carry out; affect = influence. thēe-ātre - a common mispronunciation in rural Ireland].

Northern Secetariat

A.   Northern Secretariat [From: Secret].

Refuge collection.

A.   Refuse collection. [Refuse = "Garbage" here].

Husband and wife loved **one another.**

A.   Husband and wife loved each other.

[When only two people are concerned you say **each other**. When more than two are concerned you say **one another**].

There **is** conflicting reports.

A.   There are conflicting reports.

[reports is plural, :: "are"]

The game **sprung** to life.

A.   The game sprang to life.

[If "sprung" is to be used it must have a past-participle sense i.e. "Has sprung"].

We have a **mungrel** in the barracks at this **point in time.**
A.   We have a mongrel in the barracks at this time.
[Mongrel is commonly mispronounced, esp. in rural areas 'At this point in time' is probably the most widely used cliche in Ireland, and especially by politicians].

As Minister I favour the **weaver** system for Water Charges.
A.   As Minister I favour the waiver system for Water Charges.
[Weave, Wave, and Waive are often confused, but are different].

When the Golding's lived there, they.............
A.   When the Goldings lived there, they.....
[Apostrophe denotes possession and doesn't apply here and if it did it would be outside the **s** = Goldings' as it is **plural** number].

Tsar Nicholas 11
A.   Tsar Nicholas II (the second)
[11 = eleven.   II = Roman numerals for 2].

Dropped from the Premier Div. to the First Div.
A.   Dropped from the Premier Div to the Second Div.
[You can't drop from Premier to First, as Premier = First - "Soccer Speak"].

13 + 19?   Oh, I'm not much good at **mathematics.**
A.   13 + 19? Oh, I'm not much good at arithmetic.
[Simple addition etc. is not mathematics,which is advanced].

What a wonderful place Limerick must be to live ____
A.   What a wonderful place Limerick must be to live in.
[The statement has no meaning without "in"].

He **over-**passes it **far too much** (the football)
A.   (1) He over-passes it. Or (2) He passes it far too much.

[One stress on the point being made is sufficient].

The goalie is at the edge of **he's** area.
A.   The goalie is at the edge of his area.

As Ministher I must sthress that there should be no sthrike on the sthreet.
A.   As Minister I must stress that there should be no strike on the street.
[Many rural people sound an "h" where there is none].

I know as Minister that there **has** been various leaks.
A.   I know as Minister that there have been various leaks.

The match is being played in "Jerrys" (Jerez) in Spain.
A.   Jerez, pron. Herrez (derivation of "Sherry").
[Many Irish people don't understand or pronounce foreign words]
[J is silent or **H** in Spanish, but pronounced in Portuguese].

Thank you for **speaking with** me.
A.   Thank you for talking to me.
["Speaking" is the new "in" word, but it suggests a formal address to an assembly by two people. "Talking to" is more friendly, personal "head to head"].

'If you want them to stop, don't start' - Advertisement.
A.   'If you want them to stop, don't let them start' [still wrong].
[The sense of this Ad. is confusing and incoherent and can't be corrected].

They are calling for the **outing** of the Minister.
A.   They are calling for the ousting of the Minister.

'By Killarney's Lake's and Dell's'
A.   'By Killarney's Lakes and Dells [Plural]
[Apostrophe is being misused frequently nowadays and used where it is not even required].

If they are not **thought**, they can hurt **theirselves.**

A.   If they are not taught, they can hurt themselves.
[There is no such word as **theirselves**; their = ownership, which hardly applies to "selves"].

She **never** heard the likes in a **long time**, indeed in her **entire life.**

A.   She hadn't heard the likes in a long time.
[There is typical hyperbole and exaggeration here.
"Never" is indefinite and ∴ does not agree with "long time" which is a definite and shorter period.
(s)he cannot cite her "entire life" because (s)he hasn't yet lived it. Florid, exaggerated, thoughtless language].

I **never** come here **much, nowadays.**

A.   I don't come here much, nowadays.
[Similar to the last example, confusion of senses here.
"Never" does not accord with "much" or "nowadays" which both suggest occasional visits. (Irish utterances are not always based on logic, but are usually spontaneous and undeliberated)].

'I'll be back with the 9 o'clock News tomorrow, till then, enjoy the rest of the evening!'

A.   I'll be .... till then, goodbye! Enjoy the ....!
[There is a jarring incongruity about the above greeting or farewell; it is not aesthetically pleasing to the ear, even if it is not "bad English" intrinsically]
[Why can't media people say a simple "hello" or "goodbye" - even occasionally, as in normal conversation].
The "rest of the evening" doesn't last till the next day and so falls short of a full farewell or goodbye.

A **mixture** of fear and a **mixture** of panic.

A.   A mixture of fear and panic.
[It is impossible to have a **mixture** of fear on its own, "mixture" infers more than one ingredient. What is intended here is a single mixture of **two** things, fear and panic, rather than the impossible stated two mixtures of one each].

59

Jŭdge, Jŭst, Sŭch, Does (Dŭs)

A. Jodge, Jost, Soch, Doz - phonetically
[In Connacht especially, the **u** in these words is often pronounced "soft", while the spelling remains correct. The correct phonetic sounds are given in A. above, with the spelling corrupted for effect].

The opposite is true for Pŭt, Fŏot, Tŏok, Bŏok where the vowel **is** soft, eg. book = buk not "bok".

Fíne Gael (often pron. Fyne)

A. Finé Gael (pron. Finn-eh) a Gaelic name.

It was bought **off** him.

A. It was bought from him.

This is **he's** first win, he got **beat** twice here.

A. This is his first win, he got beaten twice here.

His **disassociated** himself from it.

A. He **dissociated** himself from it.
[While the former is technically correct also, the latter is regarded as the more aesthetically correct].

Between **you** reading it and **me** talking about it.

A. Between your reading it and my talking about it.

There are so many new buildings **have** gone up.

A. Delete "There are" for a better aesthetic sense or/- There are so many new buildings (gone) up.

Q. [2 marks].   Which mountain range does the Rhine rise?

A. **In** which mountain range does the Rhine rise?
also: which mountain range does the Rhine rise in?
Although it is considered "bad taste" to end on a preposition, e.g. to, in, on, at.
[Incidentally, the answer given to the Q. was "Black Forest"!?]
- the **correct** answer was? - The Alps].

Should not treat them any different **to** men.
A. Should not treat them any different from men.
He was charged with the **robbery** of £15,000.
A. He was charged with the theft of £15,000.
[Money **cannot** be "robbed" as it has no wallet or possessions on its "person". It can only be stolen].

People should make **up** their own decision.
A. (i) People should make their own decision (or)
(ii) People should make up their own minds.
[Here is an example of a common confusion of two thoughts. The speaker meant to say either (i) or (ii) but changed thoughts or sentence, midstream. He should have finished one train of thought first, even if it was flawed. He could then correct himself in the next sentence, and clarity would have been maintained].

'Goodnight' and welcome to this Sports Special.
A. Some media presenters (Sports and Weather) esp. say "goodnight" at the **start** of their delivery. "Goodnight" is nowadays "goodbye", and should be used only at the end of a programme, as a **final** goodbye.

Your letter of the 12th **instance** (= example)
A. Your letter of the 12th instant. (present month)

'The **amount** of people, esp. women, **that** come to us'
A. 'The number of people, esp. women, who come to us'
[**Amount** and **that** refer to inanimate objects, not people].

Myself and Gerry, along with **himself** and Paul celebrated the win.
A. Gerry and I along with Paul and he celebrated the win.
[Humility, good taste and good English suggest that you put yourself last.
The above persons are the Subject(s) of the sentence.
If they were the Object, it would read: Gerry and **me**,
Paul and **him**].

He was fairly **shook** after the experience.

A.   He was fairly shaken after the experience.

["shook" is a common colloquial usage in rural areas].

Roddy Doyle **bet**rayed the **voil**ence very well.

A.   Roddy Doyle portrayed the violence very well.

Whether **or not, both** sides meet.

A.   Whether the (two) sides meet.

["Whether" infers choice, which includes the option "or not", so "or not" is superfluous and repetitive.

'**both** sides meet'. "both" is surplus to the understanding as it stresses "as opposed to one", when its obvious that **one** cannot meet].

The people in both communities **wants** peace.

A.   the people in both communities want peace.

["The people" is not normally a singular unit, but normally a collective plural, ∴ **"want"** (plural)].

There will be **no more happier** Minister.

A.   There will be no more happy Minister.

or There will not be a happier Minister.

or There will not be a more happy Minister.

City theatre not **effected**.

A.   City theatre not affected. (already analysed)

I will, as Minister, take that particular **rout**.

A.   I will, as Minister, take that particular route.

Those **way-outs,** those **ways-out.**

A.   Modern lingo is adopting "ways-out"

But the original 'way-outs' is still correct also as it recognises the hyphenated words as **one** word in sense; therefore it is right in plural number to put the **s** at the end as if **one** word, e.g. **wayouts.** Two words hyphenated = one word, therefore the plural can/is/should be an "s" at the end of second hyphenated word, as with **one** word.

62

He took the bread and āte (āat) [Hard vowel]

A.   He took the bread and ăte (et) (Soft vowel)
[Āte is an "americanism" - now accepted here.
But "et" is also still in current use].

Who are **always** as helpful **as ever**

A.   Who are as helpful as ever.
["Always" and "as ever" are duplicate and repetitive so
one of them is sufficient as they are synonyms].

They felt that their trust had been **mis**betrayed.

A.   They felt that their trust had been betrayed (i)
or/ they felt that their trust has been misplaced (ii).
[This looks like another case of "crossed wires", confusion
of thoughts or sayings or change of mind in mid-sentence.
He could have said either (i) or (ii) but he confused both
as **"mis"** should have gone with **"placed"**].

This **Phenomena** is new.

A.   This phenomenon is new (singular number)
[Phenomena is the Latin plural form (latin plurals end in **"a"**)
now coming back into vogue for the English plural of
"phenomenons". some people confuse **"a"** as singular].

Bought at the **cheapest** price.

A.   Bought at the lowest price.

On the Galway to Dublin **Rd.**

A.   On the Galway to Dublin road.
[**Rd.** usually refers to a proper noun or name e.g. of a street
or avenue in a town or estate **"Road"** as in Galway to Dublin
is a **common noun,** not a name of a **particular, individual**
street, therefore it is not abbreviated and need not have a
capital letter, unless it is a title or banner headline].

A **young** baby, and the other **kids** love **it.**

A.   A baby, the the other children love her/him.
["young" is surplus as it is understood in the word "baby".
"kids" = young goats. "it" = inanimate object or thing, not

a human being].

In the **throes** of an economic boom.

A. **"Throes"** denotes pain and anguish and is at odds with **"boom"** which denotes the opposite: success and joy].

He was **complemented** on his success.

A. He was **complimented** on his success.
[Complemented has a different meaning = to complete or join].

Unbelievable, Fantastic, Remarkable! (Adjectives]

A. These terms have come into common usage to mean "great" or "very good", but literally they don't mean either "good" or "bad" and are often used too loosely as jargon, hyperbole or exaggeration, esp. by teenagers or excitable people.

From 9.30 a.m. **in the morning** till 6.30 p.m. **in the evening.**

A. From 9.30 a.m. till 6.30 p.m.
or From 9.30 in the morning till 6.30 in the evening.
[As 9.30 a.m. is **obviously** morning there is no need to repeat it; likewise with 6.30 p.m. - duplication].

I have never **drank.**

A. I have never drunk.

The car hit a **three** in **Thrim** and five people are now **deceased**. We want witnesses to contact us.

A. ...... hit a tree in Trim, and five people are dead.
[Many Irish people (North and South) insert a "h" where it is not required; others remove it from the same words, e.g. Three (Tree) when it is required. "Now deceased" is formal, official language, stiff].

We were **both** colleagues on the Late Late Show.

A. We were colleagues on the Late Late Show.
["Both" is superfluous as it is obvious that **one** couldn't be colleagues].

The Mayor of Coventry on R.T.E. radio was asked what he attributed his "mayor-al-ity" to. He thought it was "morality" and proceeded to talk about religion, sex etc.

A.   Mayoralty (**Maerlty**) is often mispronounced in Ireland and broken up into 3 or four syllables, as proffered to the Coventry man above.

Opponents **to** the Mullaghmore prŏject.

A.   Opponents of the Mullaghmore prŏject.
[Project is often pronounced with hard stress on the vowel o, i.e.; ō, even in its noun form. It should be soft o as in "prŏd", as it is not meant to be prō as in "for"]. Verb = prō.

I don't **talk** English here, even to my fellow teachers.

A.   I don't speak English here, even to my fellow teachers.

There **are** a whole series of people on to me as a T.D.

A.   There is a whole series of people on to me as a T.D.
["Series" is a **singular** term or a group noun - collective].

He decided to **lay** down and rest (lay an egg?)

A.   He decided to lie down and rest.
["Lay" for lie is an "americanism", recently arrived here].

We are not **used of** it (Common in rural areas).

A.   We are not used to it.

The position in Irish Steel is un**teen**able (phonetically)

A.   The position in Irish Steel is untenable (ten)

In **Linster** House.

A.   In Leinster House.
[This is a fairly common habit in Connacht especially].

Leave him out [Free him].

A.   Let him out.
["Leave" is a common usage in Munster, especially].

PHONETIC SOUNDS

(Key to Pronunciation)

Vowels (hard)	ā ē ī ō ū	(mate, mete, mite, mote, mute, moot)
Vowels (soft)	ă ĕ ĭ ŏ ŭ	(rack, (w)reck, rick, rock, ruck, rook)

As in dictionaries, the mark (-) over a vowel denotes "hard" sound and the mark (˘) over a vowel denotes "soft" sound.

Vowel sounds denoted by ˘̄ may be pronounced either way; e.g. Ate (Et - European way, or Āat - American way) also 'pā̆tent', etc.

Consonants: b, ch, d, dh, g h, k, l, m, n, ng, p, ph, r, s, sh, t, tch, **th**, v w, x, y, z, zh.

The consonant **th** presents considerable difficulty to the Irish palate and tongue, especially in Dublin and Cork, where it is often pronounced as **Dor De**, e.g. Dat, De, Dem, Dose.

CHAPTER 4

THE MOST COMMON 'ERRORS' IN "IRISH ENGLISH"

De, Dis, Dat, Dese, Dose, Dem ["Th" problem]. Thee-āā-tre. In the North, the opposite tendency, e.g. "tree" becomes "Three". I pot my fot on the bok (put, foot, book). Deteriates, I **done**, I **seen**, "You know", "like". Complement (i). **Amount** of people. 'At this point in time'. "Inter-**rest**-ing" Shall I - will I. Each other - one another. Effect - affect. Harass (pron.). Ye (for you). Mode (for mood). Aren't I. Bona Fide. "Basically"; "Amazing" - guy" - "fabulous" person (Hyperbolé) Heighth. Line-outs (Lines-out). **Disected**. Disassociated. "Kids" for children. "It" for a baby. Rout (Route) Crulety. **Ec** Cetera (ect) Corps (pron. Corpse). Affect (effect). [Exaggeration:- 100,000 Welcomes]. Sink (for wash-basin) Rarin' to go. Price is to **dear**. Temperatures too **cold**. Myself and John. Foreign (mis) pronunciations: e.g. "Heloise", "José", "Marseilles". Refuge (refuse). The Ryan's were out. Whether **or not**. Referenda "Speaking with" "speaking to". Secetry (secretary). Poignant. **Terrible** nice, **fierce** fit. Up at **half-seven**. Troath (throat).

[Provincial Dialects: Connacht: **Verra**, Gineral, Linster. Munster: De, Noo (New) Millen (Million). Confusion of "s" and "z" sounds. Leinster: **Voilence**; De, Dese, I seen, I done, brudder, udder (other). Ulster: Niah (now), Till (to), I done; has **went**.]

Americanisms: I'll **lay** down on bed; Skedule. Speak with. I āte; Cool man! You're square. Man, ah will. Don't see none. Dīrect (direct). Dīsect.

BAD HABITS IN SPEECH

Repetitions: These are probably the most persistent and exasperating habits of bad speech. Unfortunately the speaker may not be aware of this, as habits tend to be subconscious. Thus it becomes ingrained and may never be corrected unless a friend tells the speaker about it.

The most common repetitions in Irish speech are: "you know", "like", "basically", "actually". These terms are used over and over every day to the point of tedium. Irish people in general don't go for deep thinking or ordered, logical reasoning, thus "you know" is often a sign of insecurity or an appeal or desire to be understood to the hearer. "You know" is a constant check to see if the listener is following the line of delivery. It can betray a lack of confidence by the speaker in his communicative ability (or in his listener).

Another term in common use is "basically". A typical practitioner is the smug, self-assured, neuvo-riche yuppie type. Similarly, a caller to a radio programme on 14/12/91 repeated 'in actual fact' thirty seven times. One of our leading politicians repeats "obviously" over and over again. Some people repeat: "personally, I think" ["personally" is superfluous because "I think" is already "personal"] [I is a personal pronoun] 'The "actual" person' is another "howler" oft incanted; "actual" adds nothing to person, place or thing, so it is superfluous, mere baggage or verbiage.

Non-Sequiturs and Half-Sentences: After "repetitions" probably the most trying habits are the "mid-sentence break-off", non-sequitors. This is the widespread practice of changing tack or sense or meaning in mid-stream, ending in general confusion all round. Paradoxically this can arise from an over-anxiety to be clear and coherent and to impress. It betrays muddled thinking and a lack of singleminded purpose. The remedy may have been unwittingly provided by Magnus Magnussen on "Mastermind":- 'I've started so I'll finish'.

Even if a better thought intrudes mid-stream, it should be held over, until the sense of idea or message or train of thought of the initial, original utterance is completed - even if it is nonsense! It can then be corrected, or rescinded even, in the next sentence, and coherence and intelligibility will have been maintained - much to the listener's advantage and ease.

Incoherence is caused not only by not finishing one's

sentences. There is also a recent innovation: politicians' gobblygook. Some cynics would claim that this is deliberate. Examples of this habit are 1) waffling. 2) avoiding the question. 3) cliches.

1) Waffle: an extended, convoluted body of verbiage but without rational content, point or purpose.

2) Avoiding the Question: This disease has reached epidemic proportions in Irish politics. An example:- Interviewer:- 'Yes or No, do you **believe** the peace is **permanent**'.
Politician:- 'I "sincerely" **hope** so!' The interviewer did not ask about his **hope**, but his **belief**.

The following is a fictional mock speech, illustrating political gobblygook: waffle, evasion, and especially "cliche".

3) Political "Newspeak":- '**We, in The Honest Party, at this point in time,** would like to **re-iterate our commitment to full employment, a united Ireland and 100% Gaelic-speaking Ireland!** As long as "**you the electorate**" - the most "**intelligent in Europe**" continue to believe us, then we won't ever have to actually **do** these things, but merely **state** them - especially **in opposition** since we won't then have to **do** anything. But now that we **are in Government** we will as usual plead '**the international political and economic recession**' as the reason for our inability to achieve these **great Republican goals of ours** (even after 50 years!?). The recession is a **world-wide phenomenon**, and totally **beyond our control!** But if you **good people** (mugs) continue to be as gullible, sorry "intelligent" as ever then we can say, **without fear of contradiction**, that we **in this great Party**, can continue with **absolute confidence**, (to fool you) well into the **new millennium**, as we have done so faithfully, **in the past**. And as we are, **according to the polls,** as popular as ever with **you the voters, we see no reason to change, as you good people** seem to continue to believe in **our promises** and prefer our **words** to our deeds. And in a thousand years, **a cháirde**, as we continue to promise you those **great national, republican** and **industrial** (and impossible!) **goals**, men will say: '**this was their finest power**' (that shower!).

Go raibh míle maith agaibh.
An Páirtí Macánta.

69

"AMERICANISMS"

These are probably the biggest threat to standard English in our time. Because of the universal reception of American T.V., films, News etc., everyone is being influenced by this "new age" English speech. It is having a corrupting affect especially on teenagers and on those who are not sure of their own language. "Americanisms" can appear more "cool, man" to impressionable minds, and standard English might seen to be "square". Schools (and parents) should list these words and phrases in class, so that students will know how to distinguish between them. Unless "americanisms" are **recognized**, they can have a distorting influence on our language, as they are very pervasive and insidious and catchy. At least if students know them for what they are then they can choose to use them as slang and for fun, while still having standard English for "normal", correct and formal use. Know what ah mean, man! So that "innocent minds" will be made aware, some "americanisms" are listed below. American T.V. can supply others:

Hi there **folks! ah āte mah grub** on **skedule** today.

A.   Hello there friends! I ate my food on schedule today.

Hi = Hello. Folks: people, friends, listeners.

Ah = I. Āte (ate = et). Mah = My.

Grub: Food. **Skedule** = Schedule (Shedule).

Man, don't **ha-rass** me. A. Har,ass (Har,ess).

Ah'll speak with mah lawyer, man!

A.   I'll talk to my solicitor.

On the sand-**doons**. A. Sand dunes.

She's **cool**, but he's **square**, but I like **'em**.

A.   She's nice, but he's old-fashioned, but I like them.

Nicklaus is still out on the **golf**-course. A. No need for **golf**.

Ah don't see **none**, there **ain't none.**

A.   I don't see any, there aren't any.

So early in the **ball**-game. **A.** "ball" is superfluous.

Take **five** man, you need to **lay** down and rest.
A.   Take a break, you need to lie down and rest.

Monday **thru.** Friday.
A.   From Monday (through) till Friday.

Bathroom (Toilet, lavatory)

45 minutes away (time it takes to drive).

Honey, I **shrunk** the **kids.**
A.   Honey, I shrank the children.

I'm in a mean **mode,** man.
A.   I'm in a mean mood, (man).

The Quarter-back **disects** the posts.
A.   The Quarter-back bisects the posts.

A common "american" innovation is the **stressing** of the first vowel sounds where they are heretofore soft or silent, especially the "i". This "unfortunately" can distort the word entirely, e.g. the "English English" word "dissect". This has been corrupted to "disect" - a new word, not in any dictionary. Also "diverse" become divers(e). Recourse (rek...) becomes Recours(e) (Ree,ko...). Ate for Ate (Et.). "Direct" becomes "direct" (Die-rekt). Consonants also have been exaggerated and have become more sharply pronounced, e.g.:- **Schedule** (Sheddule) has become **Skeddule.**

The double negative is slowly infiltrating our "system" e.g. "I **ain't no** fool".
Literally, this means the opposite of what it intends: A literal "translation" is: 'I am **not no** fool' or "I am a fool" [Is this a joke on "americanisms"?]

Muhammad Ali told a joke about his days in Kentucky. He entered a "Whites only" restaurant but was told 'We don't serve no niggers'. Ali (then Cassuis Clay) replied 'That's O.K. man, ah don't eat 'em'.

Note:- The single most common and invasive influence of "americanisms" is the hard stressing of the vowels, where they were hitherto silent or "soft", within words; e.g. Ate (et) has become Āte (a̅a̅t); Di̯rect = Dī-rect. Consonants also have become "stressed", e.g. Schedule = Skedule.

PUZZLE

Man, looking at a picture, says: "Brothers and sisters I have none
But that man's father
Is my father's son."
Q.   Who is the man in the picture?

This "simple" puzzle befuddled the nation some years ago. It was aired on a prominent Radio Show, in an effort to solve it. A University Professor was called in to adjudicate. After an initial incorrect "official" answer, the correct answer was finally given, following calls from the public. It took one week.

A.   The speaker is looking at a picture of his own **son** - not of himself, as many people say.
[Clue: 'My father's son' = me; ∴ 'that man's father' = Me]
Simple!

VULGARISMS, VICES AND VANITIES

'F_ _k off, you, you _ _ _ _' an expression heard every day.

'That is pure **crap** - Politician.

[Crap = Excrement, not used in cultured circles].
[Of course, the speaker may be unaware of its meaning].

'Two players **axed** by team selectors' - Newspaper.
["Axed" is a violent, crude and unsavoury term].

'Three new players being **blooded** for Sunday's hurling match.' -
Newspapers and Radio.
["blooded" applies to the Unchristian and barbaric practice of letting
coursing greyhounds or hunt-hounds catch hares etc. in an enclosed
space in order to give them a "taste of blood"]. And we are
"Christians"?!

The use of the name "Jesus" loosely and loudly and frequently in
conversation (e.g. 'Jayzus, is it yersell'?].

The everyday use of F_ _k, S_ _t etc. - Widespread. We seem to enjoy
comedians who use vulgar words. Are we two-faced?

Besides the verbal habits, some other common traits are:- sneering,
leering, sniggering, sniffling, snuffling, nasal snorting, spitting. The
handkerchief is no longer much used, and tissues are not used by
everyone, even when sneezing or sniffling. Despite the emphasis on
hygiene nowadays, Communion in the hand is still not universally
practised in church. Hands are not always washed "after use" in
Gents' toilets. Child abuse and cruelty to animals are other traits, as
are putting feet on seats, smoking in non-smoker company, and
litigiousness.

We don't seem to have a code of honour, in politics, business or
commerce. Romans fell on their swords, and the British resign from
office even for minor misdemeanours, but we don't voluntarily admit
error, apologise, or resign on principle, for the most part.

And on St. Patrick's Day we believe we are - an island of saints and scholars! And we crave praise and flattery.

But all is forgiven in the wealth of talent and beauty and joy and laughter...... of Irish music and dance - the most beautiful language, and sweetest national trait of all.

"Political Correctness"

This is another American innovation, now being taken to unfortunate extremes; e.g. a black-skinned person may be referred to as "pigmentally-challenged", or a road-sweep a "municipal enhancement operative". The Isle of Man may yet become the Isle of Person! [Although "Man" here is the generic/species, rather than the **male**, term].

In Ireland, "Tinkers" has become "Itinerants" and now "Travellers". This is because we have become **ashamed** of the original words. But it is not the **words** that are the problem, but our mental connotations. If "Tinker" (a worker of tin) is considered derogatory, then "Traveller" will soon become so too, as has the cultured word "Itinerant" already.

New fashions are not necessarily good fashions, and a point to remember is that the English Language was properly and soundly established, before "American" came to assault the airwaves of speech.

CHAPTER 5
HUMOUR IN IRISH SPEECH

Some of the wit in Irish "English" is deliberate; but most is "unwitting" or un-intentional, and all the better for that. The writer, John B. Keane enjoys relating the irony and sardonic wit he observes daily, and is a ready raconteur himself.

He tells of the man who travels over a mountain track to a "wake". He sees a light and approaches the humble thatched cottage and knocks. The door is opened, and he enquires:- 'Is this where the dead man lives?'

It is good to see that Irish people can laught at themselves; the following are from a chart on public display at the Ferry Terminal in Dun Laoghaire, Dublin: [From Notices and Newspaper Headlines].

1.   Man denies committing suicide.
2.   Man recovers after fatal accident.
3.   She is a female woman of the opposite sex.
4.   Persons with relatives in this graveyard are asked to keep them in order.
5.   Dead Garda in the Force for 15 years.
6.   Gardaí found safe under blanket.
7.   Danger! Touching these wires will result in death. Anyone caught doing so will be prosecuted.
8.   I'd give my right arm to be ambi-dextrous.
9.   Friday disco, exclusive; all welcome!
10.   Anyone who goes to a psychiatrist should have his head examined.
11.   Autobiography? Is that the history of cars?
12.   We had the Greenes for dinner today.
13.   Parade on Sunday afternoon. If raining then the parade will take place on Sunday morning.
14.   I don't like being taken for granite.
15.   Clairvoyants meeting cancelled due to unforeseen circumstances.
16.   Piano: would suit beginner with chipped legs.

17. Death is hereditary.
18. When the water reaches 27°C take the temperature.
19. Visitors are requested not to take flowers from any except their own graves.
20. Ears pierced while you wait.
21. Man found dead in graveyard.
22. Gardaí move in book case.
23. A bachelor's life is no life for a single man.
24. Streakers end in sight.
25. Bargain basement upstairs --
26. A lady should never crumble her bread or roll in her soup.
27. Enraged bull injures man with axe.
28. Mr. Murphy died in June 1976. Had he lived he would be buried here.
29. The accident occurred at Merrion Road as the dead man was crossing the road.
30. The Councillor said it was 'a virgin wood where the hand of man had never set foot'.
31. If he were alive today, he'd turn in his grave.
32. Kathy Kelly, 1902 - 1952. Let her R.I.P.
33. Lost: Old brooch depicting Venus in Phoenix Park.
34. The bride wore a long dress that fell to the floor.
35. Traffic lights stolen in Swords. Garda spokesman claims thieves will stop at nothing nowadays.
36. Terrier, gentle, eats anything, loves children.
37. Wood doesn't grow on trees you know!
38. In Ireland this happens 100% of the time, thats nearly always.
39. Closed for official opening.
40. The athlete was always behind before, but now, he was first, at last!!!?

There are other "Irishisms" (a) of an innocent, simple type, and (b) some which seem to be 'tongue in cheek' or deliberate.

(a)   Countryman giving directions to a tourist: 'If I were you, I wouldn't start from here at all'.

(b)   There's weather on it, I'd say, Paddy!. Bedad aye, the sky is in a bad spot alright. Tis very unsettled to be sure, there the other day now, sure, the sun was shining one minute for a few hours, and the next minute it was raining all day. Bad for the turf, no dhryin'.

True enough, Paddy, I'm thinkin' meself that its all this permissiveness nowadays, hah?

While Irish people can laugh at themselves and accept Irish jokes and enjoy themselves socially, we are not, (surprisingly) as quick or as witty or funny as the British. This is evident in the respective comedians, comedies, T.V. advertisements etc. We are still that bit too serious, self-conscious and afraid of error. An example: The presenter on a Radio 1 programme on 15/12/93 asked a caller: 'have you ever eaten a clementine? Caller said: 'Oh, yes, I have! Of course! 'What is it', asked presenter. 'Oh, I can't remember' replied the caller.

Oscar Wilde - An Anglo-Irish wit. [Unequalled]

Unlike the British, the Irish are not over-concerned about logic or plausibility in things or tales:- 'Fionn Mac Cumhaill lifted and flung a piece of Ireland a hundred miles'. [And that was before "Guinness for strength"].

An ad. says: He will now make the **girl** disappear! ... **He** is now totally invisible! [Confusion here between the subject (he) and the object (she), it seems] [Poetic licence, or a slip?].

Several other ads. are apparently flawed in logic and sense but nobody cares because we are easy-going and we allow for artistic licence, imagination and suspension of disbelief. Imagination knows no bounds here, because we bid a stranger not **one** but "100,000 welcomes" while at the same time hindering him by willing 'the road to **rise** before him'. Obviously then we are good story-tellers and fiction-writers. 'May the road **rise** before you is an Irishism gone wrong, from the Gaelic: 'Go **n-éirí** an bóthar leat' which really means:- 'may you enjoy the road' (i.e. your journey).

The following are actual extracts from students' answer papers. [The best educated young people in Europe, our politicians claim]. the students would have been mainly 16 year olds:=

1. The man's blood was **pousent,** and so killed the dog.
2. I **herd** water up **threw** the floor, **squerting** in my face when I **donc** it. I phoned the **plummer;** he came and opened a **knut** and **terned** it off.
3. Q. 5: Punctuate the following:-
   'the teacher said Séan is a fool'
   A. 'Séan is a fool because he left school before the Inter.
4. Q. Is the poet mocking?
   A. The poet is mocking, because if he was serious it would not be funny.
5. fast and **furerous** .... where I can **cloccted** (collect it)
   ..... He was not **drounded** ..... I rang the fire **bridge** ..... I sent for the **blumber** .... my fahter **layed** pipes.
6. **Tipicall** of Dickens .... We got home in one **peace.** ... the roads were **slipy** ... There must **of** been....... We were fast asleep when we heard a hissing sound.
7. .... Julia's concern for the trout shows she is very concerned about it.
   .... **Their** was no Mass that day.
   .... **Tempreatur** ..... **Smudder** to death ..... Fingers **num**
   .... not **quiet** right .... **throughing** snowballs.
8. O'Connaire wrote the poem on paper .....
   The dog had a **desire** .... I **mopth** the floor.
   ..... Stephen **excepted** the explanation given ......
   Surplys were running low ....
   the **gardes** brought us to the **barkes** ......
   The car came out of no **ware** and **slided**
   .... I slept awhile **on till** I heard a noise
9. Charles **Darwin** (Dickens) in most of his novels created characters ....
   The spider was creeping slowly but **surly**

10. Q. Show the similarities of his situation with that of the mouse.

A. Small eyes and nose.

11. Q. Give examples of fun in Pickwick Papers.

A. (a) when the women faint I couldn't stop the laugh.

(b) when your man ran out shouted "Fire" that would have been best.

12. Q. Comment on "cruelty" in Wilde's "Reading Gaol".

A. **Crulety**:- You would **no** he was against hanging, no type of people like that should be **aloud** to run prisons.

13. I have **too** good friends .... I **paniced** .... The dog was **insein** .....

I could **bearly** see .... **Look** was on my side .... Evil **figuores** for **centurys** .... He doesn't dislike the mouse, but **show** a bit of **likeness** for him instead ... Looking for **infermetion**.

14. I found the poem very funny because it was very **humerous**.

15. 'The boys discovered the nest while they were out looking for nests'.

16. 'Death on the elegy of a mad dog' - by Liam **Flaothary**

.... The **presence** of adults is **present** ... He **layed** it down.

17. Cuchulainn was real because he played hurling, and became a warrior for the King of Cullen

.... The **seen** the wren .... I had my **doughts** ....

They **done there** jobs .... They had the same similarity

.... The well had two **points** of water ....

were I come from

18. He **choosed** to live in a quiet part.

19. My father got **tick** with me.

He was so **tick** he could kill someone.

20. He killed the dog with his **bear** hands.

While there is humour in the above samples there is nevertheless a certain poignancy too, because this stunted speech and script may be carried throughout life by these people.

It is the duty of parents, teachers and the education system to ensure that priority is given in schools, from the earliest age, to language and elocution. Language must be cultivated, **before** literature or the dreaded exam. distorts the pupil's educational focus and vision:

'Literature is a luxury, desirable indeed
but language is essential, in life, to succeed'.

Some of the humour in Irish speech is evident in the
deliberately contrived or exaggerated depiction of the simple,
innocent, yet wily country-man. This monologue is often rendered
heartily and knowingly inthe West of Ireland:-

- The Countryman reporting the theft of his bicycle -

Hello, Guard, ... tis a fine day, begod, it is!

Guard: That it is, I can plainly see.
But what brings you in?

Man: My wyskel (bicycle) was shtole, I'm afraid, Guard.

Guard: Tell me about it (getting pen and paper).

Man: Well ... I got the Dole .... and I went in to Peteen Dan's Pub
for a few pints of porther, like, you know.

Guard: What time was this?

M. Well, I'd say around eleven in the mornin', like.

G. Go on!

M. Well, I dhrank about 14 pints of porther and I ate wan hang-
sangwich. When the Dole was spent I came out into the air.
I got sick then and I wommitted - in the usual place, around
the side, you know, like.

G. You spent the whole day in the pub?

M. Well, Guard, it was Dole-day as I said...... and anyway the
shky was in a bad spot and it looked like there was weather
on it and no day for the hay, and .....! Yuh know yersell, like!

G. Look, I'm not interested in that. You said you called about
your bike.

M. Oh? Oh, yes, Guard, you're right .... It was shtole!

G. How do you know?

M. Well, Guard, I always lave it around the side, near to where
I wommit and handy for goin' home, like, you know.

G. Go on!

M. Well, last night when I left Peteen Dan's, there it was, up
against the wall, gone!

G. Have you got the number of the bicycle?

M. Faith no, Guard, sure the number was shtole too!

G.	Ahem! Was it a lady's or gent's bike?
M.	Oh faith no, Guard, it was my own, I tell ye!
G.	I know, so it was a man's bike, ha?
M.	Hah? Well... It... It was a Raleigh bike!
G.	Was it black or white or coloured?
M.	No!
G.	No what?
M.	No Guard ... Sir!
G.	Look, this is impossible. I'll tell you, we have an unclaimed bike out the back now for a year and two days. Would you please take it and go - and we have the number too - its on it! Now go!
M.	Well, Goh blesh ya, Guard; sure I seen ye bringing it in a year ago, right enough, an' I knew twas shtill there, like.
G.	What! You, you!

- Politicians "Newspeak: -

(a)   You get tired shaking hands with the same old faces.

(b)   If Dev. were alive today he'd turn in his grave.

(c)   Where the hand of man has never set foot.

"Soccer - Speak"

Radio: ....'And they're the **Premier** Division results. .... Here now are the **First** Division results.... ..... After this loss Man. Utd. boss Alex Ferguson said he was disappointed that he didn't come away with a **"result"**. That's the Sports news for now goodbye'.

Andrei Kanchelskis

Son:	Dad! Dad! what does **"Premier"** mean.
Dad:	"Premier" means **"First"**, son, you should know that.
S.	And does "First" then mean "Second".
D.	Of course not, son, don't be silly. Why do you ask?
S.	These soccer results, there is no Second Division.
D.	Of course there is son, its the.... well, er... the "First Division".
S.	You mean the Second is actually the First, and the First the Premier?
D.	Well, er, yes, well no, well look son, you're too young!
S.	And is the Third Div. the Second Div. and the Fourth the Third?
D.	Look son, I'm busy!
	- LATER -
	Dad, Dad! What is a **result**?
D.	Use your head son, it means a win, draw or a loss, whatever is the final outcome of the match. Simple!
S.	But Dad, Alex Ferguson said his team didn't get a **result**, they lost 3-2 to Sheffield Wednesday today?
D.	Well son, its like this, well, I mean, well, its complicated.
S.	But you said it was simple! Dad!..... Dad!

Father, aside:- Kids! why do they have to complicate simple things? Can't they understand plain English? I blame the teachers nowadays; not like in our day!

N.B. [In Britain and Ireland the top Division in football is now called the Premier. The next Division (the second) is now call the First etc.]

Bad pronunciation and bad punctuation can be a source of mirth, but, unfortunately also, of misunderstanding and misrepresentation; e.g.

(a)   The eminent clergyman is a well-known **tinker** (thinker) -
- R.T.E. Radio.
[The presenter did not pronounce his "th"]
[He meant to say **"thinker"** but it sounded like **"tinker"**.
A tinker was a travelling dealer in, or maker, of tin cans].

(b)   The Traffic **Corpse** were alerted to the offence.

"POMES - PENNYWORTH"

FOUR TODAY

Little Caroline is 4 today!
Bright and chirpy as a bird.
Doing things around the house, (chores)
- 'Or this is what I've heard!?
Mammy's busy and Daddy works,
So Caroline says "Hello"!
Into the phone to take her calls,
From those who love her, ... So!

She knows the voices, and to each one,
She tells of all she's got; (presents)
A dress from Nola, and many more,
Although she's just a .... Tot!

Caroline will soon be big
But we'll always think of how;
She was such a happy, bubbly, chatty child;
And beautiful, then .... as now!

SWEET BABY JANE

Jane comes to visit us, just once a year;
And her sweet smile heralds, that summer is here;
A smile full of sunshine, and warmth and good cheer
To lift up our spirits, whenever she's near.

Like the coming of swallows says winter is past
And dark dreary days are over at last,
Jane comes like the summer sun's gentle sunlight,
To fill the long-golden-hours with smiling delight.

To Aran and Clifden and Lough Corrib's Isles,
Silver Strand's sands, salt, surf 'n sunshine,
Endless days' frolics, games, splashing, sheer fun,
And to sleep, still smiling, when long day is done.

Jane will grow up, blonde, beautiful and sweet,
But her greatest gift to each person she'll meet,
Will be the joy in her smile, like her granny before,
To cheer all hearts that bless her,
To God's own golden Sea-shore.

GAYBO

He is eloquent and brash and rather good-looking; (well?)
De-be-on-**air**, with poise and good carriage;
Splendid of figure, with grace and good manner;
Boyish pure glee and hearty true candour.

Gay is so loved, because he is honest;
Unpretentious; straight and kind-hearted.
With breeding and culture; class and true style;
Charm, wit and voice, fit to beguile.

Internationally, he's admired and is courted;
But is customs-stamped to be not exported.
To this decree is the nation consented.
If he didn't **be**, he'd **be** ... **Invented!**

He is therefore, unique and quite special,
All housewives' dear and darling own "treasure";
He doesn't age, he must **always** be,
Life would have no spice, if **he** were not **He!**

He is not too deep, rather is light and **GAY!**
But is never afraid to have his own say.
He doesn't pretend, or feign, to high knowledge,
Yet masters debate on Church, State, or College.

A patron of Arts - to the Festival Dome,
The escort the Roses really **would** like to take home.
All "mothers' pride", grannies, daughters, to wit,
Elegant eligibility, Man, just **IT!!**

And still n' all, he's just 'wan of our own' (y'know, loike!);
A neighbour's son, from ould Sth. Circular Road.
He loved his mammy, he ne'er broke the rules;
He's a shining example for all C.B.S. schools.

They want him for President, T.D. or Saint;
But trammelled by pride or passion he ain't.
His true crowning glory, that no one can spurn;
Is that he's just **Himself**, the one and only **Gay Byrne**.

CONCLUSION

The author hopes that this book will have been of some interest and help to those who are students of good English; - and of some enjoyment to those who are expert!?!

 All of the quotations given are actual and true, as heard or read by the author. Names are not given, as the purpose of the book is educative. If the author has erred in quotation or correction then he apologises. The text is not expert or definitive, but merely the observations and opinions of one person only, albeit a secondary school teacher of English, based in Ireland.

 As the purpose of the book is **educational**, its contents are not meant to parody, ridicule or defame anybody. Imaginary or fictitious samples could have been given, but the author felt that actual, authentic quotes would be of more interest to the reader. The humour cited is not mocking but intended as balance and light relief to the serious text.

 The "errors" cited here are not peculiar to politicians, radio/T.V. people or newspapers, but are characteristic of the Irish as a people or culture, whose native tongue was originally mainly Irish or Gaelic or Gaeilge. The author also is Irish and is therefore within that same national milieu, - "like, you know"!

ACKNOWLEDGMENTS

To: Three doughty teachers of English who proof-read the
        manuscript of this book.
        [This is not to say that the book is without error, in fact,
        inference, reference, or conclusion].

For: The filial faith, forbearance and forgiveness of Persons,
        Parties, Parliamentarians, Pressmen and Public Broadcasters
        whose parlance might have been partially and imperfectly
        parsed, particularly!   Pardon;   please!

For: Pictures published here, which are copyright of their sources.

INDEX